utb 5245

utb.

Eine Arbeitsgemeinschaft der Verlage

Böhlau Verlag · Wien · Köln · Weimar
Verlag Barbara Budrich · Opladen · Toronto
facultas · Wien
Wilhelm Fink · Paderborn
Narr Francke Attempto Verlag · Tübingen
Haupt Verlag · Bern
Verlag Julius Klinkhardt · Bad Heilbrunn
Mohr Siebeck · Tübingen
Ernst Reinhardt Verlag · München
Ferdinand Schöningh · Paderborn
Eugen Ulmer Verlag · Stuttgart
UVK Verlag · München
Vandenhoeck & Ruprecht · Göttingen
Waxmann · Münster · New York
wbv Publikation · Bielefeld

Dr. Vera Leberecht, PhD, studied Linguistics, Intercultural Communication and Theology in Germany and Finland. In her dissertation, she analysed the communication in university professors' office hours. Being a certified trainer for academic writing, she worked at Maastricht University Language Centre for several years as an instructor and section head. In 2008, she started her own business as a trainer and coach. She works with people in academia and beyond who want to communicate with reason and resonance.

Vera Leberecht

Teaching in English in higher education

strategies – tips – support

Narr Francke Attempto Verlag Tübingen

Umschlagabbildung: © EtiAmmos – stock.adobe.com

Bibliografische Information der Deutschen Nationalbibliothek
Die Deutsche Nationalbibliothek verzeichnet diese Publikation in der Deutschen Nationalbibliografie; detaillierte bibliografische Daten sind im Internet über http://dnb.dnb.de abrufbar.

Dischingerweg 5 · D-72070 Tübingen

Internet: www.narr.de
eMail: info@narr.de

CPI books GmbH, Leck
Einbandgestaltung: Atelier Reichert (Stuttgart)

utb-Nr. 5245
ISBN 978-3-8252-5245-8 (Print)
ISBN 978-3-8385-5245-3 (ePDF)
ISBN 978-3-8463-5245-8 (ePub)

Contents

How to use this book

Personally, I find the best way to use books is to read them. Of course, this is only true for good books. But then, you usually only know whether a book is a good book after you have read it. As I have great confidence in my readers' professionalism *and* common sense, I trust that you will find out quickly whether this book is worth your time. Like many of its fellows, it could simply be read from front to back as it has a structure the author has chosen on purpose; likewise, you could skip parts and directly dive into the sections that address your most urgent needs and wants.

Above all, I hope that you approach this book with an open mind and a willingness to learn and be surprised. If you actually enjoy yourself for a moment or two while reading this book, I would be happy to have reached one of my main goals.

1 Introduction: What this book wants and is – and what it is not

Congratulations! You have just taken another hurdle on your way of becoming a better lecturer in your discipline in English. You think I am exaggerating? Quite honestly, I think so, too. It is just that every book needs a first sentence, and this was the first sentence that came to my mind when I wrote this paragraph.

Having admitted that, I can honestly say I *do* believe you have taken a hurdle. After all, you have just made it through the first paragraph of a book on teaching in English in higher education, and this might feel like a first, if small, success. If it does, you are on the right track; if, in contrast, this is already starting to bore you, and you find yourself thinking where else you could look for more substantial input on teaching in English, this book might not be the right resource for you. In this case, feel free to pass it on to a colleague and continue your professional journey on a different path.

If, by now, you are still not quite sure whether it makes sense for you to continue reading, the next few pages are for you: They will let you know whom I address and what I intended when I wrote this book; they also provide a short preview of each chapter, so you know better what to expect.

So for whom have I written this book? I imagine that you resemble the participants in my workshops on teaching in English who typically work as professors, lecturers, or instructors at universities and universities of applied sciences in Germany or its neighbouring countries. I suppose you would describe yourself as someone who

- is a more or less competent and experienced professional in their academic discipline,

- is more or less experienced in teaching, supervising and supporting students in higher education, and
- more or less enjoys teaching their subject matter (I *do* hope you go for the "more" option in this case!).

And I am probably on the safe side when I suppose that you are a member of the fast-growing crowd of teaching staff in higher education who have more or less recently been confronted with the glad – or not so glad – tidings that they are expected to share their knowledge with their students in English. If you have not been involved in international cooperations for decades or were lucky enough to grow up in a plurilingual family, you may initially have been shocked or, at least, slightly surprised and insecure; you may have wondered whether the relics of your high-school English would suffice to keep your students in the room for the duration of a complete lecture or seminar session. On the other hand, you might be one of the many European instructors in higher education who are pretty comfortable about teaching in English and just would like to refine their skills and competences. If you can relate to any of the above characterisations, this book has been written for you.

This takes us to the next question: What do I intend with this book? The answer is simple: I want to encourage you. As stated on its cover, this book provides strategies, practical tips, and support for English-medium higher education. It aims to equip you for taking your own steps of putting English-medium teaching into practice at your own pace and in ways that suit you and your institutional contexts. Gradually, you can expand your comfort zone of sharing your expert knowledge in a language that is neither your own nor most of your students' first language.

Let me underline it once more: This is a book about practice. It is a direct outcome of more than a decade's work with practitioners teaching at tertiary-level institutions in European countries with other official languages than English. Many of its topics have been shared by and discussed with workshop participants. As a result of this hands-on focus, many issues related to English-medium teaching in higher education have *not* made their way into this book: It does not give an overview of the current research and theory on English-medium instruction (EMI). It does not deal with theoretical considerations and concepts of content and language integrated learning (CLIL) or English as a lingua franca (ELF). If you would like to learn more about the theoretical foundations of teaching in English in higher education, you will find other books that are more suitable than the one you are holding in your hands. To get you started, I have put suggestions for further reading at the end of many chapters of this book.

What can you expect from this book? Chapter 2 sets the scene with prerequisites for becoming more competent and confident about teaching in English in academia. Obviously, when I talk about prerequisites, I do not mean diplomas or certificates but helpful attitudes and competences you acquire as you teach and communicate with students and colleagues in and outside the classroom. Each of the four subchapters of chapter 2 is complemented by hands-on suggestions for developing and applying these prerequisites.

Chapter 3 broadens the horizon further. It starts by depicting the manifold experiences of lecturers who have been on the road of English-medium teaching for a while. These experiences show that challenges and difficulties with switching to English as a medium of instruction in higher education are far from individual. The chapter provides a lot of questions as well as space for notes and reflection. This is to encourage you to think about your own answers, and to discuss these issues with superiors, colleagues, and students.

Chapter 4 is one big plea for using clear, simple, plain English in lectures and seminars. This aspect has made it into a separate chapter because, to me, it is one of the major differences between many continental European academic traditions and cultures and their Anglo-American counterparts. The chapter provides some statistics, theoretical considerations, and practical strategies, so you can decide which approaches will be most appropriate and useful for your own student audiences and communicative goals.

Leaving theory behind, chapter 5 provides tips and activities to handle the daily chores of English-medium teaching in higher education more effectively and efficiently. It includes ideas for activating students and for using writing as well as some online resources.

Finally, chapter 6 provides glossaries with useful words and phrases for communicative situations in English-medium teaching. They include general academic vocabulary as well as language for classroom management and oral exams, to make sure you will never be speechless again.

I hope that this brief overview leaves you with the impression that there is *very little* magic about switching to English as a medium of instruction and that you have long been familiar with many, if not all, of these topics, ideas, and phrases. Like in many other areas in life, for things to work, you simply need to put into practice what you know. Are you ready to do that? Then let's go!

Further reading

Ball, P., Kelly, K., & Clegg, J. (2015). Putting CLIL into Practice. Oxford: Oxford University Press.

Coyle, D., Hood, P., & Marsh, D. (2010). Content and language integrated learning. Cambridge: Cambrigde University Press.

Dearden, J. (2015). English as a medium of instruction – a growing global phenomenon. London: The British Council. Retrieved from www.britishcouncil.org on 15 August 2019.

Fortanet-Gómez, I. (2013). CLIL in Higher Education. Towards a Multilingual Language Policy. Bristol/Buffalo/Toronto: Multilingual Matters.

Gundermann, S. (2014). English-medium instruction: modelling the role of the native speaker in a lingua franca context. Doctoral dissertation, Albert-Ludwigs-Universität Freiburg.

Lawrence, C., Inbar-Lourie, O., & Weinberg, K. (2017). A Handbook for English-Medium Instruction in Institutions of Higher Education in Israel. Retrieved from https://tempus-ecostar.iucc.ac.il/wp-content/uploads/2017/05/EMI-BOOK-ATAR.pdf on 15 August 2019.

Mehisto, P., Marsh, D., & Frigols, M. J. (2008). Uncovering CLIL. Content and language integrated learning in bilingual and multilingual education. Oxford: Macmillan.

Wächter, B. & Maiworm, F. (eds.). (2014). English-Taught Programmes in European Higher Education: The State of Play in 2014. Bonn: Lemmens. Retrieved from www.aca-secretariat.be/index.php?id=792 on 15 August 2019.

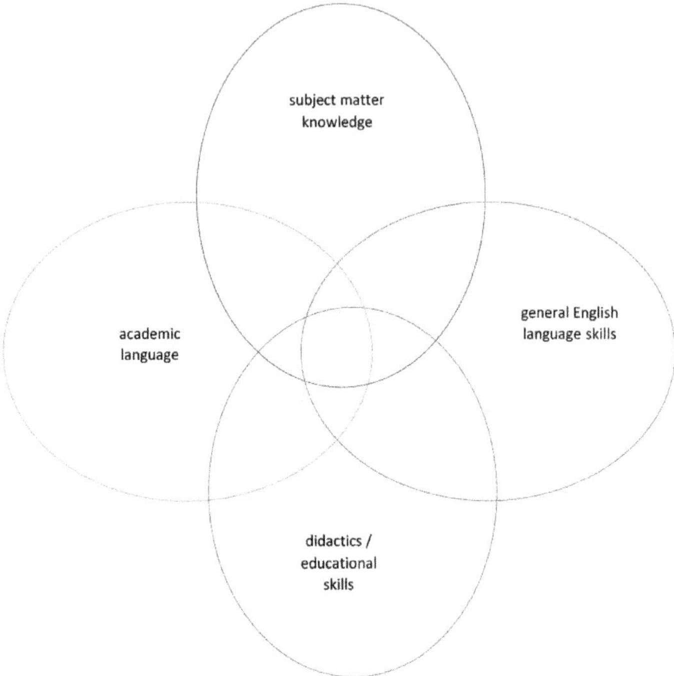

English-medium teaching: areas of expertise

2 Making it work: What is needed to succeed in English-medium teaching?

When you ask me what I think is the most important factor for succeeding in English-medium teaching, I can answer quickly: practice. I firmly believe we become better English-medium teachers by simply going into the classroom and doing it. I know *extremely* few people – and I am sure you do not know many either – who have learnt to ride a bike by looking at other people on bicycles, by talking, reading or writing articles about it, by creating theoretical models of cycling and presenting them at conferences or, even, by writing blogs about cycling or watching online video tutorials. The same is true for teaching in English: We learn it by doing it. And this does not change when we call the whole thing "embedded social practice".

Now I can almost hear you object: 'But I know this! Why do you state all these things that are completely obvious?!' Well, that is probably because I agree with Erich Kästner, the well-known German writer, who once said that knowledge alone does not turn people into good teachers.[1] I am convinced that you know most, if not all, of the things I have been saying on the previous pages; and this may not change much as you continue reading. However, especially in professional contexts, we sometimes make choices intuitively without being aware of whether they are useful, and why. Therefore, every now and then, we are well-advised to step back and reflect on

- the choices we have made,

1 Admittedly, Kästner put it more generally and lyrically ('Es gibt nichts Gutes, außer man tut es.') One English equivalent of this aphorism is much more prosaic but also makes the point: 'Wishes won't wash dishes'!

- what we have learnt from these choices, and
- whether the competences or skills we have acquired as a consequence of these choices are still the ones we need, or
- how we could expand our knowledge and develop our skills in other, more efficient and effective ways.

Hence, I invite you to be open for some food for thought, and for becoming an *even better* teacher of your subject in English.

Lecturers who attend my workshops sometimes expect that they will turn into confident, fluent, near-native speakers of English in one day. Of course, that is not how it works. Mastering a language takes time, practice, and many opportunities to speak without being afraid of making mistakes. But it does not end there. I see way too many individual lecturers who are burdened with the responsibility of making English-medium teaching work. Yet, not individuals but whole institutions of higher education are responsible for ensuring that their teaching and adminstrative staff and their students are provided with structural, professional support for learning the language (cf. Hochschulrektorenkonferenz 2011). And there are more issues that deserve attention. The following four areas need to be dealt with, early and profoundly, if English-medium teaching in academia is to become more than a one-semester hype:

1. subject matter knowledge,
2. general English language skills,
3. didactics / educational skills, and
4. academic language.

The next sections look more closely at each of these areas.

References and further reading

Hochschulrektorenkonferenz (2011). Sprachenpolitik an deutschen Hochschulen. Empfehlung der 11. Mitgliederversammlung der HRK am 22. 11. 2011. Retrieved from www.hrk.

de/uploads/media/Empfehlung_Sprachenpolitik_MV_22112011.pdf on 15 August 2019.

2.1 Subject matter knowledge

Your interest and expertise in your subject matter are probably the foremost reasons why at a certain point in your career (last week, or many years ago) you suddenly found yourself in front of a group of students, trying to share with them some of the things that interest and fascinate you.

I assume that you have spent most years of your professional career acquiring and expanding your subject matter knowledge. Depending on whether you are affiliated to a university or a university of applied sciences, and depending on your discipline (used here in the sense of "academic specialisation", *not* your willingness to work hard), this will have happened to varying extents within and outside academic settings.

Certainly, you are aware of the fact that to teach your subject matter in English, you need to know what you are talking about. In our context, let us focus on the language element of this endeavour. In other words, I want to draw your attention to terminology, i.e., subject-specific terms and phrases: To teach your subject matter, you need to understand it, *and* you need to be able to use the correct words to share your knowledge, understanding, and expertise.

Depending on your specific field of research, you may feel comfortable about reading English texts – or not. Over time, you may have turned into a more (or less) experienced writer of research-related genres such as papers, articles, conference abstracts, grant proposals, a doctoral dissertation, habilitation thesis, etc. In sum, both your passive and active knowledge of English terminology may be considerable, whether you are aware of it or not.

In addition, by pursuing an academic career and having survived it to this day (more or less successfully and happily), you must have proven that you are able and willing to study. So here is the good news: As you are facing the challenge of sharing your content expertise in English, the first thing you need to do is simple: Learn the words. Study the terminology. Master your subject's vocabulary.

No, this does not happen overnight – or within a one-day workshop. But there is no magic about it either. It just takes some time and focused effort because you already know *how* to do it. You *just* need to *do* it. Here are some ideas, or reminders, how you could approach this (with thanks to numerous colleagues and former workshop participants):

- Read English textbooks, books, papers, journal articles, and professional blogs on your subject. The trick here is to "take off your content glasses" and to "put on your language glasses" every now and then; with that, I mean that you focus on language and style rather than content, and that you pay attention to familiar and new words that you could use in your own teaching. Maybe you even want to take notes. Decide how you profit most from this kind of professional reading.
- Search for online and offline dictionaries, glossaries, and databases on your subject. They are invaluable (which, somehow paradoxically for non-English speakers, means *very* valuable!) sources of professional development for English-medium teachers.
- Watch videos on your subject: Many universities in the Anglo-Saxon world provide online lectures and training courses. When these courses are aimed at students, you can use them as examples of how first-language speakers of English present their contents. The courses aimed at instruc-

tors might provide useful tips on good lecturing in addition to the subject terminology.

- Attend international conferences and proactively use them as stages for presenting your research. Expand your small-talk competences in coffee breaks and at conference dinners, and you might come home with a new English joke or two in your repertoire …
- Start writing your own blog, or look for opportunities to contribute to existing blogs as a guest writer. This is a good way to practise reaching out to students, fellow researchers, and interested readers in the general public.
- What about setting up international cooperations, working groups, or research projects at your university, or breathing new life into a collaboration or project that has been fading away in a remote corner of your department for a while? Maybe a cooperation with a company or research department in another part of the world would be a logical spin-off from one of your culturally diverse classes with Erasmus students or other international students? Or could you benefit from the professional contacts of a visiting or guest lecturer? The fact that English is used in workplaces all over the world opens doors to many regions where people are used to communicating in English and are eager to cooperate internationally. Many smaller countries, e.g., the Benelux and Scandinavian countries, have long traditions of using English and are often able and willing to liaise with interested individuals or institutions. The German Academic Exchange Service (Deutscher Akademischer Austauschdienst, DAAD) provides information on opportunities for individual and institutional cooperation (www.daad.de/hochschulen/de/ (in German; last accessed on 22 August 2019). Inspiration for and information on specific international cooperations can be found on many universities' websites.

- If you are looking for something that requires less commitment than setting up a complete cooperation programme and pays off in the short term, you could involve your students in a brainstorming session to explore which strategies would be useful to expand both your own and your students' active terminology. Who said that you are solely responsible for vocabulary/terminology development in your class? What about joining forces to create a glossary? When you emphasise that students are responsible for developing their command of subject terminology, you may also raise their awareness for ensuring that everybody in class uses the terminology accurately and consistently. Maybe creating a glossary, or contributing to it, could even be a part of the grade your students receive?
- Finally, become a networker: Share your experiences, be they pleasant or awful, and interview colleagues who are a few steps ahead of you on the path of English-medium teaching about *their* failures and successes. Find out which strategies have worked for them, and be open for activities and approaches that may not have worked for others but might be just right for you.

Whatever you decide to do to develop your subject terminology, make sure you start soon and take steps – big or small – regularly.

Time for reflection:

What can I do to expand my English subject terminology?

Which practical steps can I take by the end of this week to get me going?

Please allow me one final remark here: Yes, expanding your subject terminology takes time. But remember, whatever language you decide to learn takes time. And, in a way, the terminology of your field of research is yet another language. To master it, most of us will have to make an effort, and need to practise. But this experience can bring us closer to our students who are usually facing not only this single challenge, but a whole load of them: They do not just have to learn some new English words but also come to grips with the principles, methods, theories, models, contents, and researcher identities these words represent! So regardless of the language in which you share your subject with students, never forget that *you* are the expert! Your students are usually aware of that and perceive you as exactly that: the expert. It might feel awkward to have students in your class whose general English language skills are much better than yours because they were born in Canterbury, Connecticut, or Canada, or have recently returned from an exchange year in Northern Ireland. But remember: You are the one in the room who knows much more about fluid dynamics, the autopoietic reproduction of social systems, or robotics than they do – and that is exactly why they attend your class.

2.2 General English language skills

While it is essential for English-medium teachers to know their subject terminology, terminology alone will not help you to make it through a 90-minute lecture or seminar – *and* to keep your students from dozing off or running away. You will need a certain level of fluency in what is usually referred to as general language, too.

I sometimes talk to lecturers who are experts in their fields of research and have accumulated many years of teaching experience but are still insecure about switching to English-medium instruction. They usually state that they feel restricted in their use of humour or idiomatic expressions when they switch to English; this, they say, prevents them from expressing themselves authentically and invitingly. This always reminds me of a colleague who one day decided to make real work of his use of humour in his English-medium course. He started spending some of his preparation time on thinking about, or even actively searching for at least one joke, one humourous remark or one metaphor; he would look up the correct English wording, and put down in his notes where exactly he would use it. Usually, he learnt the joke by heart; sometimes, he included the exact wording in his notes. Before you frown on such tedious work that *must* kill each sparkle of spontaneity, I would like to remind you that many experienced professional speakers who give enthralling presentations do this all the time – and, of course, actors and comedians spend a lot of their time off stage doing the same. Even though they may seem to be extremely spontaneous, full of ideas, and totally relaxed sputtering out all those funny ideas coming to their minds at that very moment, all these professionals are far from leaving that to chance. In particular, most speakers to whom every word seems to come so naturally, spend many hours on rehearsing their performances. There is nothing despicable about practising how to start or finish a lecture in a foreign language. It might make you feel a bit – or more than a bit – like being an absolute beginner again, and most of us do not enjoy that feeling. However, when you switch to English as a medium of teaching, in a sense, you *are* a beginner again. Letting go of unrealistic expectations and giving yourself the time to learn and adapt can be a relief. As you work on enhancing your general English language skills, you might find that you profit from strategies, competences, and contents that go beyond your academic research interests. Here are a few suggestions; get inspired and go along with what works best for you:

- Read English-medium books, newspapers, journals, blogs, cartoons, etc. We are living in times when you can find information on almost every topic on earth online, much of it for free; and new and second-hand books are easily accessible. Why not go for the English original every now and then instead of waiting for months until the translation is released?
- Watch films, series, and documentaries on television, streaming services or other channels in English rather than in translated versions. Turn on the English subtitles so you understand unfamiliar accents or fast speakers. At the beginning, you may find it difficult to grasp the nuances. But once you have got used to the strange sound of your favourite actresses' (own!) voices, you might find yourself enjoying the subtle linguistic humour that often gets lost in translations. By the way, watching subtitled television is very likely how most of your Scandinavian and Dutch students have become proficient speakers of English.
- Listen to English media as often as possible. If you travel a lot or have other time slots in your daily or weekly schedule that you can spend listening to the news, or informative or

entertaining programmes, why not explore new podcasts and audio books?

- Use learning software or apps to brush up your English. As little as a few minutes per day, or several times a week, can help to build a routine. Try different providers and programmes to find which fit your expectations, language level, and availability, and then stick with them. Regular exercise is key.
- Go back to school. Of course, you could be bold and ask your superiors for funding to go to South Africa, South Carolina, or Southampton for an intensive immersion language course. If they think you exaggerate, they might still be able to provide funding for a refresher course at your own institution of higher education or the local adult education centre, so you can revise the grammar and practise fluency.
- Seek individual language support. You may not be thrilled by the prospect of sitting in a class with a bunch of other people who have completely different language problems and questions. In that case, treat yourself on some individual sessions with a competent language coach. This enables you to discuss topics you are really interested in, and to receive tailored on-the-spot language feedback. Even a few individual language coaching sessions can boost your progress and motivation.
- Find real first-language speakers of English. If you are not able, or willing, to pay a language professional, you can still look for opportunities to get involved in international clubs or other settings, either online or in the real world (if anything like that exists in your hometown …). There are so many people with so many interests on this planet that you certainly will find someone to communicate with in English. Maybe you just need to take one step out of your comfort zone? Try acting in an amateur drama group, singing in an

international choir, learning a new game, or joining a sports team. In most places with institutions of higher education, the options are almost endless.

It hardly matters *what* you choose to do to improve your general English language skills and fluency – as long as you take a first step and begin doing *something*. This is not about being original; it is about looking for opportunities to practise, and to become more confident. Which ideas do you have? Which specific steps could you take to get you beyond the stage of high-flying New Year's resolutions, and to make speaking English a habit, or even a pleasure?

Time for reflection:

What could I do to practise my general English language skills?

What are practical ways to incorporate more reading, speaking, and listening to English into my daily, or weekly routines?

What will be my first step and when exactly will I take it?

If you are eager now to explore various possibilities to improve your general English language skills, fine. If you are not, that is fine, too. While it is good to work on strengthening your language skills, let us not overestimate their importance. Remember: You do not study English to pass an exam. You only revise some basic language and grammar issues and get some fluency practice in order to make yourself understood in the classroom.

However, there is one exception: If you realise (from student or peer feedback, for example) that you have an accent that makes it literally impossible for students to understand you, you need to take action. The same holds true for speaking difficulties that have psychological or physiological reasons, such as lisping, speaking extremely softly, or losing your voice quickly. Of course, such difficulties can also cause problems in your first language; but they might increase under the pressure of performing in a foreign language (cf. Hellekjær 2010). If you intend to stay in a job that includes speaking in public regularly, you are well-advised to work on your speaking skills and pronunciation with a language teacher, communication coach, or speech therapist.

References and further reading

BBC (2019). Learning English. Retrieved from www.bbc.co.uk/learningenglish/ on 30 August 2019.

British Council (2019). Learn English. Retrieved from www.britishcouncil.org/english on 30 August 2019.

Hellekjær, G. O. (2010). Language matters. Assessing lecture comprehension in Norwegian English-medium higher education. In: Dalton-Puffer, C., Nikula, T., & Smit, U. (eds.). Language use and language learning in CLIL classrooms. Amsterdam/Philadelphia: John Benjamins. 233-258.

United Nations World Food Programme (2019). Free Rice. Retrieved from www.freerice.com on 23 August 2019.

2.3 Didactics / educational skills

Unlike primary and secondary school teachers, most novice lecturers and instructors at institutions of higher education in Germany and other continental European countries do not receive any comprehensive training. The vast majority of them are not prepared for the challenges of teaching, testing, and assessing. Rather, they are thrown in at the deep end.

Mastering at least *some* educational skills in addition to their subject matter is essential for academic teachers who are serious about creating effective teaching and learning spaces for students. Of course, this is true for *all* teaching, regardless of the language of instruction. Thorough didactical training for tertiary education has been treated as a stepchild for too long. Wonderfully, the decision to switch to English-medium instruction often puts this issue into the spotlight: As more and more decision-makers and teaching staff are expected to approach teaching *in English* structurally and professionally, they realise that great teaching skills do not fall into our laps on graduation day. Discussions on the requirements and standards of professional English-medium teaching draw all stakeholders' attention to the importance of continuous professional development for teaching *in general.*

As I am writing this, the number of comprehensive, high-quality staff development programmes tailored to the needs of teaching staff at German universities and universities of applied sciences is rising. Here are some starting points for an online research to give you an idea of the possibilities in various regions in Germany:

- https://www.diz-bayern.de/zertifikat-hochschullehre-bayern (for staff teaching at universities of applied sciences in Bavaria);
- http://www.profilehreplus.de/zertifikat/ (for staff teaching at Bavarian universities);

- http://www.bzhl.tu-berlin.de/menue/unser_angebot_fuer_sie/berlin_certificate_of_teaching_internationally/ (for staff teaching at universities of applied sciences in Berlin);
- https://www.faszination-lehre.de/info/zertifikat/ (for staff teaching at universities of applied sciences in Brandenburg);
- http://www.hd-mittelhessen.de/zertifikate.cfm (for staff teaching at universities and universities of applied sciences in Hessen);
- www.hdw-nrw.de/zertifikate (for staff teaching at universities of applied sciences in North Rhine-Westphalia).[2]

Apart from the professional networks mentioned here, many institutions of higher education have set up their own certificate programmes. Particularly if you are still early in your career, go for all the training you can get! If your institution offers such a certificate programme (no matter in which language): Attend a course, or the whole programme, get to know new teaching methods, find inspiration, share experiences with colleagues, and do some networking. You might find the following online materials and course offers useful, too:

- The British Open University (www.open.edu/openlearn/) offers many free courses and materials for continuing education and professional development. For a search focusing on educational issues, you could start on www.open.edu/openlearn/education or www.open.edu/openlearn/education/professional-development-education, using keywords such as "education career", "learning to teach", or "higher education".
- The Open University also offers degrees and courses for international students; they can be found here: www.openuniversity.edu.

2 All websites last accessed on 22 August 2019.

- The British Council, in cooperation with the BBC, provides resources for continuing professional development on www.teachingenglish.org.uk/teacher-development/continuing-professional-development. The section on 'Using multilingual approaches' combines issues of subject and language teaching. You may have to browse a bit to find materials that are useful for higher education; however, many of the ideas for secondary education can be transferred to academia.[3]

Of course, there are also myriads of books on the topic. Here are some of my favourites for getting started:

- Barbara Gross Davis' 'Tools for Teaching' ([2]2009) is an inspiring resource book for teachers in higher education. It is packed with practical, easy-to-apply ideas for all areas of academic teaching. At the same time, it is well structured and clearly written. This makes it a useful companion for your journey of becoming a more confident teacher of your subject matter in English.
- Anthony and Karen Haynes' (2012) revised and updated edition of the classic '53 interesting things to do in your lectures' is part of a series that provides practical tips for professionals in academia in a very accessible manner. The '53 interesting things' range from structuring teaching processes and content to fostering and assessing student learning. The tips are presented in a pick-and-choose format and can easily be transferred to various lecture formats and situations.
- Hannah Strawson's '53 interesting things to do in your seminars and tutorials' (2012) works the same. It covers structuring sessions and dealing with written materials as well as evaluating student achievements. A lot of attention is paid

3 All websites last accessed on 22 August 2019.

to encouraging and facilitating group work, and student participation and responsibility.

Obviously, in *English-medium* teaching situations, you may meet challenges that are not covered by these books aimed at academic teaching staff in general. Chapter 5 discusses strategies to activate students in situations where understanding might be limited due to language difficulties of both teachers and students. However, there is one strategy I would like to draw your attention to here and now: *embracing redundancy*.

Switching to a second or foreign language of instruction is likely to make it more difficult and time-consuming for many students to learn and understand a subject matter. Therefore, many English-medium teachers find it useful to not just *accept* redundancy as a necessary or even annoying by-product but to welcome it happily and use it purposefully. This makes even more sense when we consider the conventions that prevail in most Anglo-Saxon academic discourse communities (cf. Reid 2010, 17): Writers (or, in our context, speakers) are responsible for framing the information and conveying it in a way as structured and simple as possible so that readers/listeners can absorb it without thinking too much; readers/listeners more or less expect to be 'spoon-fed the information'. As a US American saying on academic writing, cited by Reid, says: 'First you tell them what you're going to tell them; then you tell them; then you tell them what you told them.' (ibd., 18).

If you consider such an approach too childish for tertiary education, I would like to stress again that we are dealing with *culturally diverse expectations of what constitutes professional academic communication* here. It is your decision: How much attention do you pay to these differences in your own course preparation and class? Do you explicitly talk about these differences with your students, who may be struggling, or do you let your students find their own ways to deal with them? Which cultural/academic/disciplinary traditions do you come from and which ones do you cultivate? You can do your students a great favour when you discuss such cultural differences and share your personal perspectives and ways of dealing with them.

Practically put, what can *embracing redundancy* look like? Actually, you do it whenever you talk and show a powerpoint slide at the same time. In some disciplines, it is common to orally elaborate on an idea, definition, or model while writing it down on the blackboard, whiteboard, smart board, or flip chart. In other disciplines, teachers hardly ever do this or would not even consider it. That is a shame because writing something down and talking simultaneously a) forces you to slow down and b) gives you time to think and formulate, or reformulate your ideas. It can also make you more aware of how much time and concentration it takes most students to take notes, to listen to you, and to understand what you are saying, all at the same time! So even if talking and writing simultaneously is not a common teaching strategy in your discipline, you may want to look for ways to experiment a bit and see what works for you and your students.

Haynes and Haynes (2012) stress the importance of embracing redundancy (even in first-language lectures!) and list multiple forms of being redundant to enhance understanding. Their practical, simple suggestions include

- repeating briefly what you did last week and giving a short teaser about next week's lecture to provide more overall orientation so students get an idea of the bigger picture.
- progressive structuring: Instead of saying once and for all at the outset how the complete lecture is structured, you could reveal its structure in stages as you develop the topic. Experiment with different approaches and forms of presentation

to find out what suits your general subject matter, particular lecture topic, and audience.

- repeating information verbally to slow down the pace of your lecture, and to provide orientation through signposting. To give an example, 'instead of saying, "The next thing is (d) ..." and diving in, you can repeat what has been covered so far: "So now we've looked at (a), (b) and (c), and we can now go on to (d)"'. (Haynes & Haynes 2012, 63).
- repeating information visually by using the same diagram, graph, or illustration several times during one lecture or over the course of several lectures. You could do this while repeating information verbally, or instead. It is likely to literally deepen your students' *insight* into a topic.
- using several visual aids simultaneously. Think of combining flipcharts, chalkboards, whiteboards, interactive whiteboards / smart boards, overhead projection, slide shows, and powerpoint presentations (cf. Davis [2]2009, 433 ff.). This is particularly useful when you want to
  - illustrate complex ideas,
  - provide several alternative explanations, interpretations, or conclusions, or
  - present definitions as well as examples that students should relate to these definitions.

Try different channels to convey information in ways that suit you, and your subject matter, and remember the strengths of good old analogue teaching. Conquer back your blackboards, and use whiteboards and flipcharts. Do not let your students in the dimly-lit last rows of the lecture hall get lost in smartphone conversations while you hurry through your numerous presentation slides! If you are lucky enough to have note-taking students in your course, be aware that they have to divide their attention over looking, listening, and note taking. (We will get back to this in chapter 5.2.1.) If you write something by hand every now and then during your lecture or seminar instead of designing slides beforehand, this will automatically slow down your pace of speaking (because you will probably find it difficult to speak and write in English simultaneously, too!). It will help you to be more present and relate more to your audience. And while you model writing something down, you give your students time to write, too.

It all comes down to this: We are well-advised to refrain from trying to squeeze all the content we would usually cover in a first-language lecture into its English-medium equivalent. Rather, think about ways to *reduce* the amount of information you would like to convey, and to use multiple presentation channels. This can be a hard and painful process that may leave you with the frustrating feeling that you are hardly scratching the surface of your fascinating topic. But it is likely to affect your students' motivation and learning curves in positive ways.

For more strategies and activities to engage students in the interactive play of teaching and understanding, go to chapter 5.1. However, whichever teaching method or approach you choose, remember that being a good teacher in academia is not primarily about applying techniques. To master the 'craft of teaching', it is often more important who you *are* than what you *do* (cf. Eble ²1988).

Time for reflection:

What can I do to broaden my repertoire of didactical/educational skills in general?

How can I develop my skills and competences for teaching in English?

Which strategies can I apply in my current courses to embrace redundancy, reduce information, and ensure I get my message across?

Is there anything else worth exploring regarding my didactical skills and competences?

References and further reading

Ashton, S. & Stone, R. (2018). An A-Z of Creative Teaching in Higher Education. London et al.: Sage.

Dafouz Milne, E. & Llinares García, A. (2008). The Role of Repetition in CLIL Teacher Discourse: A Comparative Study at Secondary and Tertiary Levels. International CLIL Research Journal, 1(1), 50-59. Retrieved from www.icrj.eu/11/article4.html on 15 August 2019.

Dafouz Milne, E. & Nuñez Perucha, B. (2010). Metadiscursive devices in university lectures. A contrastive analysis of L1 and L2 teacher performance. In: Dalton-Puffer, C., Nikula, T., & Smit, U. (eds.). Language use and language learning in CLIL classrooms. Amsterdam/Philadelphia: John Benjamins. 213-231.

Dale, L. & Tanner, R. (2012). CLIL Activities. A resource for subject and language teachers. Cambridge: Cambridge University Press.

Davis, B. G. (²2009). Tools for teaching. San Francisco: Jossey-Bass.
Eble, K. E. (²1988). The craft of teaching: A guide to mastering the professor's art. San Francisco: Jossey-Bass.
Eidinger, A. (2016). A Guide to Online Resources for Teaching and Learning in Higher Education. Retrieved from www.unwrittenhistories.com/a-guide-to-online-resources-for-teaching-and-learning-in-higher-education/ on 24 August 2019.
Haynes, A. & Haynes, K. (2012). 53 interesting things to do in your lectures. London: Professional and Higher Partnership.
Reid, N. (2010). Getting Published in International Journals. Writing Strategies for European Social Scientists. Oslo: NOVA, Norwegian Social Research.
School of Teacher Education (2018). Classroom Management Guide. Retrieved from www.unco.edu/cebs/teacher-education/undergraduate-programs/classroom_management.aspx on 24 August 2019.
Strawson, H. (2012). 53 interesting things to do in your seminars and tutorials. London: Professional and Higher Partnership.

2.4 Academic language

Now that we have covered subject matter knowledge, general language skills, and educational skills, the time has come to consider the fourth pillar of successful English-medium teaching: academic language.

With academic language, I refer to what most lecturers mean when they tell me they "need to broaden their vocabulary" to teach more effectively in English – or before they can even start! I have already mentioned this (real, or felt) need in chapter 2.2: In my experience, this problem is far less serious than perceived by many of these colleagues. Instead, I would like to argue that what they experience is that their active vocabulary is not as broad as their passive vocabulary. In other words, whereas they understand most, or all words when they read English publications in their fields of research, or listen to a presentation or lecture, they feel restricted when they speak or present in English themselves.

This issue deserves attention. However, I would suggest that this feeling of limitation might not be associated with vocabulary in the first place. Rather, it might result from the fact that many academics in Germany and other European countries simply lack the *routine* of teaching in English, which obviously means that *when* they do it, they are not able to behave as naturally and confidently as in their first-language courses.

Remember that in order to "function" in the English-medium classroom, you do not need to know by heart, or actively produce *every* existing expression and phrase for *every* possible teaching situation. Instead, give yourself the time to take one step at a time and to become more and more confident as you move along.

Academic word lists can be useful starting points for expanding your general academic vocabulary. The following online resources include word and phrase lists as well as suggestions how to use these lists for vocabulary development:[4]

- The academic word list (AWL) compiled by Averil Coxhead (www.victoria.ac.nz/lals/resources/academicwordlist) is an extremely useful tool, as it is organised in ten sublists that list 570 general academic words according to their frequency. Sublist 1 includes the most frequent words while sublist 10 includes words that are seldomly used.
- If you would like to work with the AWL in a structured way (or encourage your students to do that), the University of Birmingham provides additional information on the list, exercises to practise the words, and suggestions for integrating teaching academic words in your courses: https://canvas.

4 More online resources and glossaries for English-medium teaching are listed in chapter 5.3.

bham.ac.uk/courses/12947/pages/vocabulary-and-the-academic-word-list.

- The website www.vocabulary.com provides several lists that take the AWL further. To find examples, definitions, annotations, and how the words are used in different disciplinary contexts, go to www.vocabulary.com/lists/218701. Another compilation focuses on aspects of examinations and assignments, so if you are looking for words to express more clearly what you expect from your students, or why you have given them a particular grade, this might be helpful: www.vocabulary.com/lists/388513.
- John Morley at the University of Manchester has created the Academic Phrasebank (www.phrasebank.manchester.ac.uk) for academic writers; it is a useful resource for spoken academic communication, too.

Obviously, to expand your academic vocabulary, *and* to use words and phrases appropriately, instead of learning them by heart, or encouraging students to do so, it is a good idea to first ask yourself what exactly you want to do: Do you want to define terms or give examples? Do you want to explain, compare, or contrast? And how do you want your students to process what you present? One tool that facilitates this kind of reflection is Bloom's Taxonomy. Developed as early as the 1950's, it distinguishes and classifies learning objectives, assignments, and assessments according to their levels of complexity and specificity.

In our context, I am not interested in the justified objections against this model.[5] Rather, I would like to draw your attention to the potentials it has for vocabulary development. As Krathwohl

5 Critics say, for example, that the Taxonomy is too mechanistic and inflexible, and that it implies that those cognitive competences that are labelled as less complex are also seen as less valuable. In contrast, in some cultures and academic disciplines, "intellectually less complex"

(2002) points out, the Taxonomy was developed as a tool that would not only enable teachers to determine particular learning objectives, activities, and assignments but also facilitate broad, interdisciplinary discussions about learning, teaching, and assessing. Does it not come in handy that all these activities and processes are inseparably connected to language? As soon as we reflect on and make explicit our intuitive decisions and implicit assumptions, we are in the middle of language development and fluency practice!

Bloom's Taxonomy distinguishes three domains of teaching and learning:

- the cognitive, or knowledge-based domain (that looks at factual, conceptual, procedural, and metacognitive knowledge);
- the affective, or emotive-based domain; and
- the psychomotor, or action-based domain.

The cognitive domain is divided into six levels, going up in complexity:

- remembering,
- understanding,
- applying,
- analysing,
- evaluating, and
- creating.[6]

The website www.bloomstaxonomy.org/Blooms%20Taxonomy%20questions.pdf gives examples of keywords and questions

skills, such as remembering, recognising, and recalling words, images, musical notes, or facts, may be valued highly!

6 For the sake of completeness: This is the revised Taxonomy (cf. Krathwohl 2002). Bloom's original has a reverse order and slightly different labels for levels 5 ('synthesising') and 6 ('evaluating').

to deal with content on the different levels, and more verbs and resources are listed in chapter 6.1.

Obviously, being clear and concise about your subject matter and making sure that the input you provide in your lectures and seminars matches what you expect and assess in your assignments is important regardless of the teaching language. However, when the language of instruction is a foreign one for many people in the classroom, it is vital that instructors use the correct words to avoid confusing or discouraging students. Make sure that you are precise and consistent.

Time for reflection:
What are my strengths regarding general academic language? How can I put these strengths into practice and develop them?

Which strategies can I use to broaden my active English academic vocabulary and to practise fluency?

Which situations have the *highest* priority for me regarding my command of academic language? Which issue do I need to work on *most urgently*?

References and further reading

Anderson, L. W. & Krathwohl, D. R. (eds.). (2001). A taxonomy for learning, teaching, and assessing: a revision of Bloom's Taxonomy of educational objectives. New York: Longman.

Biber, D. (2003). Variation among university spoken and written registers: A new multi-dimensional analysis. In: Leistyna, P. & Meyer, C. F. (eds.). Corpus Analysis. Language Structure and Language Use. Amsterdam / New York: Rodopi. 47-70.

Bloom, B. S., Engelhart, M. D., Furst, E. J., Hill, W. H., & Krathwohl, D. R. (1956). Taxonomy of educational objectives: Handbook 1: Cognitive domain. New York: McKay.

Coxhead, A. (2006). Essentials of teaching academic vocabulary. Boston: Thomson Heinle.

Krathwohl, D. R. (2002). A revision of Bloom's taxonomy: An overview. Theory into practice 41(4), 212-218.

McCombs, B. (2019). Developing Responsible and Autonomous Learners: A Key to Motivating Students. Teacher's Modules. Retrieved from www.apa.org/education/k12/learners.aspx on 24 August 2019.

Ravitch, D. (2010). Edspeak: A glossary of Education Terms, Phrases, Buzzwords, and Jargon. Alexandria, VA: Association for Supervision and Curriculum Development.

Schmitt, D. & Schmitt, N. ([2]2011). Focus on vocabulary: Mastering the Academic Word List. White Plains, NY: Pearson.

Wilson, L. O. (2016). Anderson and Krathwohl – Bloom's Taxonomy Revised. A succinct discussion of the revisions to Bloom's classic cognitive taxonomy by Anderson and Krathwohl and how to use them effectively. Retrieved from https://thesecondprinciple.com/teaching-essentials/beyond-bloom-cognitive-taxonomy-revised/ on 24 August 2019.

2.5 Tying it all together

This chapter has looked at four areas of expertise that constitute successful English-medium teaching. To bring the loose ends together, would it be a good moment now to discuss your thoughts and ideas with one or several colleagues? It might also be sufficient for you to realise in the solitude of your home office that you already *do* know most of the things you need to know in order to convey your message to your students this semester. Maybe you realise you could have used more elegant or elaborate words but that would have served your ego more than your students' learning outcomes! (We will get back to the academic key virtue of being clear and concise in chapter 4). However, you might also have started to feel that you still have a *long* way to go... But this is how learning new skills and competences, and becoming more mature members of specialised discourse communities work, is it not? It is a process – and you are on your way.

And ... action!

The things I want to remember from this chapter include:

These are things I want to change or try:

When and where will I put this into practice?

3 Teaching in English in academia: the bigger picture

So far, we have been treating English-medium teaching as something that exclusively concerns individual lecturers and their students. However, switching to English as a medium of instruction in tertiary education involves many more stakeholders: Institutions' directors, managers and boards, politicians and legislative organs share the responsibility for making this endeavour succeed.

This chapter explores the multiple facets of our topic in two steps: Section 3.1 presents experiences, thoughts, insights, and ideas by many colleagues involved in teaching in English that I have collected in workshops, at conferences, and in personal conversations. Section 3.2 provides a truckload of questions. Teaching in English is not an issue for which there are simple, one-size-fits-all answers; it needs to be developed, negotiated, and renegotiated with superiors, colleagues, and students. The questions can serve to start fruitful, solution-oriented discussions.

3.1 Challenges and opportunities: mapping experiences

I am sure that many of the real – and perceived – challenges and opportunities of English-medium teaching mentioned on the next pages will sound familiar to you. We will move from pains and gains for teachers (3.1.1) to the students (3.1.2) and to institutional perspectives (3.1.3).

3.1.1 Pains and gains for teaching staff

What detains lecturers from embracing English-medium teaching with enthusiasm? What frustrates their colleagues who, in a weak moment, were careless enough to embark on this adventure? Here are their answers.

Not surprisingly, the biggest disadvantage, or challenge, that teachers mention most often is the time issue: Lecturers find it difficult to find suitable textbooks or other written materials, and most of them agree that preparing classes in English takes them *considerably* more time and is more work-intensive. Due to an often lower level of shared understanding during classes, many teachers spend more time on individual consultations with students outside the classroom, too. The higher workload is a particular problem in courses that are set up parallelly, i.e., when teachers are expected to offer the same amount of content, once in their first language and once in English. While it may sound easy, fair to students, and desirable from an institutional point of view, this approach loses sight of some fundamental differences between first-language and foreign-language teaching and learning (such as a slower speaking pace in the foreign language, the need for more time to explain "untranslatable" words or concepts, students being less able, or needing more time to understand the subject matter, etc.). Consequently, teachers are burdened with problems reaching far beyond their personal responsibilities.

Regarding issues directly connected to language, most lecturers indicate that they lack English vocabulary and are, thus, unable to express exact meanings, subtle differences, details, or emotions. This limits them in creating an agreeable classroom atmosphere and makes them feel less comfortable or authentic than in first-language teaching situations; some even say they feel like actors. They are restricted, and even insecure at times, as they cannot use humour as a didactical technique, or share their knowledge and skills in appropriate, helpful ways. Finally, depending on the subject matter, there might be words or concepts that simply cannot be translated. Sometimes, content gets lost, or might get lost; it remains unclear who is responsible for deciding which contents need to be covered and what could be left out. After all, in the foreign-language classroom, instructors have to divide their attention over content *and* language.

Language barriers, often combined with culturally diverse backgrounds of teaching staff and students, or among students, can lead to misunderstandings, or no shared understanding at all. Students have (more or less) limited communication abilities and (more or less) heterogeneous language levels. Moreover, teachers need to take into consideration students' different discourse traditions, cultures, and experiences as well as their expectations of adequate communication in academic contexts, or hierarchical contexts in general. For example, students may not take the initiative to ask questions or speak up in class but may have to be explicitly invited to be critical, ask questions, take part in discussions, or give presentations.

As teachers encounter increasingly diverse student populations, they are confronted with intercultural and diversity issues for which they are not equipped sufficiently, or backed up by their institutions. Sometimes, they are lost as to what is appropriate or "politically correct".

"Surface matters", such as lacking fluency, reduced speaking pace, teachers' *and* students' accents that complicate communication, grammatical mistakes, etc., are only the tip of the iceberg: Under the surface, there is a complex interplay of challenges: dealing with content *plus* language *plus* diversity plus… All these factors work together so that even lecturers who are *not* prone to perfectionism can feel more insecure than usual when they are expected to provide high-quality English-medium classes. And this often goes hand in hand with feeling left alone by institutions.

Considering all these troubles, why do many academic teachers find teaching in English worthwhile anyway? Actually, they see many direct gains for themselves: First, the possibility to use a broader spectrum of textbooks brings new insights and more diverse perspectives, and it opens doors to research beyond national and first-language boundaries. Second, as the pressure increases to consider international publications, English-medium lecturers become more aware of, and more up-to-date on, recent developments in their fields. Third, as they need to keep their teaching as clear and simple as possible, they experiment more with different forms of teaching; this is particularly true for methods to activate and enable students to take part in discussions and other interactive tasks. Last but not least, in classrooms where neither the teacher nor most students communicate in their first languages, an atmosphere of life-long learning is fostered almost automatically; teachers reveal that they are learners, too, and that making mistakes is inherent to learning processes.

However, the benefits for English-medium teachers go far beyond the seminar room and affect them more broadly as human beings: Although most of them would not say that they are bringing their hobby to the workplace, many agree that learning about cultural diversity, and practising their intercultural and language skills in real-life situations give them personal fulfillment, pride, and confidence. Apart from becoming more open-minded, they develop a habit of relaxing and letting go of perfectionism, as they realise they do not need to know all the answers in the classroom, or beyond.

In the long run, staff who teach in English (often in addition to their first languages) in higher education see this as an important investment into their professional development, as it strengthens their international profiles. Even beyond the advantages of doing research in English, lecturers who adopt English as a medium of instruction become much more flexible in working with diverse, heterogeneous student populations at home and abroad. Their horizons regarding international job opportunities are broadened, and the threshold towards teaching abroad is lowered substantially. As they become more comfortable about communicating in English, they feel empowered to actively participate in international academic exchanges, to network and to cooperate in global contexts, without being afraid of talking or listening to first-language speakers of English.

3.1.2 Pains and gains: the students' side (as perceived by their teachers)

Of course, lecturers are not the only ones who are challenged when the medium of instruction changes. Students face challenges, too. Many of these difficulties become obvious for teachers in classes where students have to distribute their attention over content *and* language, especially in the first semesters. Indeed, it may be *much* more difficult for students to grasp the content of a lecture than it would be in a first-language teaching environment. As they often do not receive structural language training, or content and language integrated courses, this is a real risk that teachers have to consider and try to reduce by adapting their teaching styles, etc. For example, many students have poor language levels, little fluency practice and limited active vocabulary at entry. Teachers have to put a lot of energy into initiating in-class discussions because students simply do not dare to speak in public.

Yet, similarly to the teaching staff, students, too, are often left alone by institutions and held responsible for dealing with the additional challenges caused by studying in English. Teachers fear that, ironically, instead of becoming proficient in *two* languages, students may put *both* languages at risk: Students could adopt or copy their teachers' or fellow students' language mistakes and perpetuate them in groups without language experts or first-language speakers who are confident, mature, culturally open, and extravert enough to correct peers or even someone in a hierarchically higher position.

Language barriers – be they perceived or real – are not the only reasons why students stay silent in class; the combined task of mastering a new subject matter and a foreign language can be overwhelming. Moreover, diverse cultural backgrounds and learnt communicative behaviours might even foster misunderstandings.

Students' cultures and countries of origin will most certainly affect many aspects of how students behave and live in and outside the classroom. This includes how students approach an academic study, deal with elders and hierarchically higher people, speak up in groups, take critical stances, report other people's ideas and opinions, etc. Often being without comprehensive support for learning the language of the host country, international students may be forced to live in an English-speaking "cocoon" without being able to take root in their environment beyond the campus. As a result, an artificial "academic tribe" emerges whose members may have lived, studied, and worked in several countries but never had substantial contact with local people, languages, and cultures. Many institutions of higher education still need to invest more money and time to offer information and side programmes in English for international students who come on short-term exchange programmes or for their complete academic careers. Otherwise, students struggling with culture shock might lose courage and drop out.

Finally, as students in English-medium study programmes struggle with integrating content, language, and cultural differences, it is possible that they need more time to graduate. This, in turn, would also mean that they start their careers – and making money – later than their peers who study in their first languages.

In this case, studying in English would actually turn out to be a real economic disadvantage, at least in the short run. As English-medium teaching is often advocated as preparing students better for international work places and equipping them with competitive advantages for the labour market in general, this might be an interesting research issue.

Bearing all this in mind, which areas do academic teachers identify where students can *profit* from English-medium instruction? Evidently, many advantages for students resemble those for teaching staff. However, teachers see specific advantages for the young academics and future researchers, too.

As English-medium courses in institutions increase, student numbers *and* the diversity of student bodies rise as well. With students from different backgrounds, nations, cultures, and ethnicities in one class, more diverse ideas, views, and experiences are brought into the classroom; this broadens students' perspectives on the subject. In addition, English-medium teaching facilitates international cooperations between institutions of higher education and companies across national borders, and even on different continents. It offers new perspectives and opens doors – virtually and literally – to academic insights, studies, institutions, and employment. Students get the opportunity to practise English in academic real-life settings. Ideally, throughout the process, they overcome their fears of making mistakes, and adopt a positive attitude towards life-long learning. Eventually, the matter-of-fact use of English in daily academic life can lead to more open-minded, confident, and interculturally competent students, thus qualifying them better for interesting jobs and making them more attractive for employers on job markets all over the globe.

3.1.3 Pains and gains for academic institutions

The challenges for institutions of higher edcuation that switch to English as a medium of instruction range from simple organisational issues to fundamental questions.

Many academic teachers involved in English-medium teaching get frustrated when they do not feel supported by their institutions. Educational institutions are often reluctant to allocate adequate preparation time and financial budgets (e.g., for English textbooks, reference books, access to databases, and other resources, both for individual teachers and for libraries, language centres, and similar service departments). In addition, there are hardly any language classes for lecturers, no editing services for course materials, no intercultural training, etc. Teachers' discontent is usually amplified by bureaucratic and organisational problems, e.g., when guest lecturers or exchange students cannot access online platforms and other institutional infrastructures, or receive insufficient training and support in English for using these resources. It often seems as if institutions attract international staff or students without considering the many issues beyond the classroom that arise when staff and students become more diverse. For example, institutions have to provide information on fundamental organisational aspects, rules and regulations for increasingly diverse audiences in English – exclusively, or in addition to other languages. Institutions should also consider their responsibilities for dealing with cultural values, expectations, assumptions, and behaviours, or even traumatic experiences; approaching such issues professionally could range from offering advice, training, and counselling for staff and students to investing in digital and analogue infrastructures.

It is also important for institutions to be clear and honest about their real offers of English-medium courses. Problems arise when students from overseas are attracted to study in Europe, move here, and then end up being disappointed by the limited number of courses the institution of their choice *actually* offers in English. If institutions of higher education are serious about English-medium instruction, they should ensure a professional, comprehensive, long-term course offer. Many lecturers feel that individuals are held responsible for this: Only few colleagues take part in the transition to teaching in English; it seems to be perceived as an individual "hobby", whereas institutions and superiors are reluctant to invest in exchange, peer feedback, team teaching, and intervision. Instead of offering additional training and support for staff who are not used to, able to, or simply *willing* to use English, institutions accept such behaviour without sanctioning it. This is perceived as unfair by those, often younger colleagues who are asked, or even commanded, to offer courses in English. At the same time, it may not even be openly discussed whether teaching in English makes sense at all in a particular region, institution, or discipline. Paradoxically, this way, institutions of higher education who want to attract *more* students may even risk *losing* local and regional students who prefer to study in a region's first language.

Many institutions may possess the political will to become players on the international stage by offering English-medium courses and programmes. However, like many other lofty aims, this can only be reached when real people do the tedious day-to-day work. For institutions to successfully provide English-medium higher education, they need to invest in resources and in staff who are willing and skilled to

- turn great ideas into reality,
- produce written information,
- organise side programmes for incoming students in English,
- offer support for studying, reading, and academic writing in English, and to
- work on creating an international institutional culture.

Language centres and writing centres that provide services, support, group and individual training for students, researchers/teachers, and administrative staff should be set up, staffed, and maintained with a sense of sustainability; yet, these important facilities are often forgotten in the exciting phase of falling in love with the idea of English-medium instruction.

Despite all these difficulties, lecturers see many advantages for institutions to switch to English as a medium of teaching, too. They know from experience, or expect to witness soon, that as teaching in English plays an increasingly prominent role, whole institutions become more international, more intercultural, gain higher reputations in international rankings, and increase their potentials to improve existing course offers. It works both ways: Institutions with English-medium course offers compete on more international markets and have to make an effort to stay competitive; in turn, higher numbers of competent researchers/teachers from international labour markets are attracted to work at internationally oriented institutions.

If an institution's English-medium course offer becomes *and stays* attractive, not only the student numbers might increase; the qualifications of graduates might be perceived as higher, too, both by the students themselves and by future employees. As students develop a sense of ease towards cultural diversity, they are better equipped for many 21st-century workplaces. When universities and universities of applied sciences put English-medium teaching high on their agendas and prove they are serious about internationalisation and globalisation, they can improve their public image and strengthen their position in the world of higher education.

Time for reflection:
Looking at the experiences and views in this chapter, what are *my* thoughts? Where do I experience, or evaluate, things differently? Where do I doubt, or disagree with the presented statements? Where do they overlap with my personal experiences?

Which specific steps can – or should – I, my department, and my institution take? Which issues deserve to be discussed and taken further?

3.2 Challenges and opportunities: taking inventory

Having looked at *other* people, I now invite you to focus on the challenges and opportunities that teaching in English brings for *you*, and to take inventory, reflect, and make your own choices. This section asks many questions that refer to difficulties as well as benefits of teaching in English in higher education.[7] How could you deal with these questions most effectively?

Like in the previous chapters, I encourage you to take some personal reflection time every now and then as you read the

7 I am grateful to my former colleague at Maastricht University Language Centre, Robert Wilkinson, for his insights and his tireless commitment to investigating and promoting CLIL in higher education; our years of fruitful cooperation have shaped and deepened my understanding of English-medium instruction considerably. Much of this chapter is based on Bob's ideas.

following pages. In addition, your English-medium teaching could profit from the questions in this chapter when you

- discuss them with students for a few minutes at the end of a lecture,
- discuss them with a colleague over a cup of coffee,
- put them on the agenda of department meetings and university committees,
- plan a department training workshop,
- look for ways to combine teaching with research into content and language integrated learning (CLIL) / English-medium instruction (EMI), or
- keep the discussion alive, both in academic publications and social media beyond the academic world.

If you feel overwhelmed by the mere number of areas covered, just start by picking the one that appeals to you – or disturbs you – most. Some of them may not concern you at all, due to personal or institutional circumstances. The topics are arranged from individual to institutional to societal ones. As many of them are interconnected, some of them might overlap.

3.2.1 The teachers' side: individual challenges and issues

Which challenges are *you* confronted with? Which challenges do *you* need to deal with most urgently and what can and will *you* do to meet these challenges?

Time for reflection: teachers' individual challenges and issues:
Are my own language skills (terminology, general language, educational language, academic language) adequate? Do I feel prepared for teaching my subject in English?

Are teaching materials available in English? If not, who is responsible for producing them? Which time and other resources, if any, are made available for developing them?

Do I have enough time for preparation and, if needed, practice and additional training? Do I have the additional time that may be needed for grading student work in English? May I have to drop other classes or change the focus of my teaching offer to make time to prepare my classes properly? How can I communicate my needs to colleagues and superiors? Is there any room for negotiation?

Am I able to provide appropriate, helpful feedback on student work in English? Who is responsible for content feedback, language feedback, etc.? Can I delegate any responsibilities for feedback to colleagues (e.g., language teachers or writing centre staff), or students themselves? If so, how can I empower them to work effectively with self-assessment and peer feedback?

Are students expected to hand in written work as part of their grades in my English-medium courses? Am I sufficiently equipped to assign, support, supervise, and grade academic/scientific writing tasks in English?

Who can I turn to for help and support for my English-medium teaching tasks? Which opportunities to network do I have in my department, with other departments, beyond my university, or internationally?

3.2.2 Integrating the teaching of content, language, and academic skills

Chapter 2 has dealt with the prerequisites for successful English-medium teaching separately. But what about the complex interplay between these areas? And what about the students?

Time for reflection: integrating the teaching of content, language, and academic skills:
Who teaches language: content teachers or language teachers, or both in team teaching? Is language taught explicitly at all, or are students expected to "absorb" it somehow automatically?

Who is responsible for teaching students academic communication skills such as

- asking questions,
- discussing and debating,
- giving presentations,
- efficient and effective reading,

- using libraries and searching for information, and
- academic writing in the discipline?

Who is responsible for supervising students, and is any training provided for this task? Who assesses students' written assignments? On which aspects do content teachers give feedback? How are they trained to do that?

3.2.3 The students

Depending on the subject matter, your research focus, your institution's location, history, course offer, marketing, and student acquisition strategies, etc., your English-medium classes may attract quite different students than your other courses.

Time for reflection: the students:
Who are the students I work with in my English-medium classes? Are they different from the students in my other classes? How?

How will my students' backgrounds, experiences, and expectations affect my work? What about their

- ages,

- nationalities, cultures, and religions,
- first languages,
- levels of English,
- motivations to study,
- previous education experiences (education systems, cultures, and traditions),
- previous work experiences, and
- life situations (family, health, residence permit, etc.)?

3.2.4 Cultural and diversity issues

Issues connected with culture and diversity are often hidden under the surface of actions and interactions; sometimes, they *seem* to be language problems, and only on closer inspection do their real dimensions become obvious. Therefore, they deserve to be considered carefully.

Time for reflection: cultural and diversity issues:
Who deals with students from abroad? How are these staff members trained in languages, intercultural skills, etc.? How do academic, administrative, and advisory staff liaise with each other to support students as effectively as possible?

How are cultural differences and stereotypes dealt with?

Are culture-specific, diverging views on plagiarism, teacher authority, teaching and learning styles, etc., made explicit? How are they treated in classrooms and on institutional levels?

3.2.5 Human resource management

If institutions of higher education do not just want to have a quick flirt with internationalisation but take English-medium instruction seriously, they will have to spend considerable time and resources on developing long-term strategies and plans, and on ensuring these plans are implemented sustainably. Professional, purposeful human resource management (HRM) plays a crucial role here.

Time for reflection: issues for HRM:

Regarding the current situation, how are content teachers' language skills assessed, and how are content teachers equipped and trained to teach their subject matters in English?

Which consequences do lecturers face who refuse to be assessed or to attend training courses?

Which incentives are there for lecturers to teach more classes in English? Which additional financial, time or personnel resources (e.g., student assistants, research assistants or administrative staff) are provided for teachers who are willing to switch to English-medium instruction?

Regarding international personnel development, how are new teachers, researchers, and administrative staff recruited?

How is our institution as a workplace made attractive for international teaching staff? Which efforts are made to attract competent researchers/teachers, taking various cultural and language backgrounds into account?

3.2.6 Institutional policy

While professional HRM is an important component of a solid English-medium instruction programme, institutional responsibilities go further than that. Implementing *and* maintaining high-quality programmes should not be left to chance, or to a handful of motivated employees. To make a lasting impact, bottom-up and top-down approaches need to be combined; processes will take time, a lot of trial-and-error, sharing, and learning from experiences both in and outside the institution.

Time for reflection: institutional policy:
To start with,

- ▷ have the fundamental arguments for and against switching to English-medium teaching been debated in and across all involved departments?
- ▷ at our institution, does it make more sense to take an institution-wide approach, or are there good reasons to adopt different strategies in different departments?
- ▷ are staff motivated to support the idea, *and* to do the tedious daily job of teaching in English?

- are financial and personnel resources made available for setting, meeting, and maintaining high standards?

Regarding explicit, *written* standards or policies of internationalisation and English-medium teaching,

- do they exist within and across departments?
- how have they been created?
- how has consensus about them been reached?
- who has been involved in formulating them and how?
- using which procedures and via which channels have they been discussed, drafted, and disseminated among all stakeholders?
- how are they adapted and updated, if necessary?
- how flexible are they?

Regarding administrative staff,

- are they expected to work in English, and what support, if any, do they receive?
- who is responsible for producing internal documents (memos, minutes of meetings, etc.) and external documents (exam regulations, websites, marketing materials, etc.) in English?

Regarding language issues,

- is there a consistent language policy for the whole institution, or have different departments adopted different strategies? Who takes these decisions and what are they based on?
- does the language policy include aspects of fostering, or even making use of staff members' and students' plurilingual and pluricultural competences?

- ▷ is there a well-equipped language centre?
- ▷ are courses in general academic language and discipline-specific terminologies offered regularly?
- ▷ does the university offer professional editing and translation services, or funds so staff and students can turn to external providers of such services?

Regarding support for academic writing,

- ▷ is there a writing centre that offers courses and individual support in English?
- ▷ are writing centre staff and peer tutors trained to work in English?

3.2.7 Higher-education policies and legal matters

To finish this chapter, here are some issues that go *far* beyond individual English-medium classrooms and even institutions. National and international policies regulate and impact lecturers' daily decisions on teaching in English, while many lecturers may not even be aware of that.

Time for reflection: general higher-education policies and legal matters:

Are there national, or European/international, political intentions and policies that affect my institution's decisions on English-medium teaching?

How are standards formulated that incoming students from inside and outside Europe have to meet?

How can these standards be reinforced?

Are there entrance tests that test the language proficiency of prospective students?

Are there any legal constraints?

Are there other policies, regulations, or laws that need attention?

Hopefully, by now, you have got a clearer picture of the many facets of English-medium teaching in higher education; you may have had the opportunity to discuss some of your thoughts with colleagues, superiors, students, and professionals at your own and other institutions; you may have exchanged ideas with people outside academia; you may have registered for a language course or started teaching classes in English. Whatever steps you have taken so far, I am sure you are ready now for the remaining chapters of this book that focus on practical aspects of language use in English-medium teaching.

Further reading

Bertaux, P., Coonan, C. M., Frigols-Martín, M. J., & Mehisto, P. (2010). The CLIL teacher's competences grid. Retrieved from http://tplusm.net/CLIL_Competences_Grid_31.12.09.pdf on 30 August 2019.

Frigols-Martín, M. J., Marsh, D., Mehisto, P., & Wolff, D. (2011). European Framework for CLIL teacher education. A framework for the professional development of CLIL teachers. Retrieved from www.ecml.at/Resources/ECMLPublications/tabid/277/ID/35/language/en-GB/Default.aspx on 30 August 2019.

Hoffman, E. & Verdooren, A. (2018). Diversity competence. Cultures don't meet, people do. Bussum: Coutinho.

Wilkinson, R. (2013). English-medium instruction at a Dutch university: challenges and pitfalls. In: Doiz, A., Lasagabaster, D., & Sierra, J.M. (eds.). English-Medium Instruction at Universities: Global Challenges. Clevedon: Multilingual Matters. 3-24.

4 Teaching in plain English: Keep it simple!

This chapter has just one message: When you teach in English, keep it simple. Why? Because you are a teacher, and teachers typically want to share their knowledge and passion so that others learn something, do they not? To reach this goal, simple language is key. Albert Einstein is supposed to have said: 'If you can't explain it simply, you don't understand it well enough'. I think this is an interesting way to look at teaching. And I would like to add that teaching has a lot to do with encouraging and empowering students. So '[d]on't make people feel stupid. Drop the jargon!' (Bay 2017).

To back up my plea for using plain, simple English in class, I take two steps. First, I argue for clear, simple communication by drawing your attention to two questions: Who is likely to attend your English-medium class? And what do different discourse communities consider to be clear, goal-oriented communication? Second, I zoom in on language. Paul Grice's Cooperative Principle and the Plain English Campaign will hopefully provide you with useful ideas for your next English-medium class.

If you are still not sure whether it is a good idea to strive for clear, simple language in higher education, the following facts and figures might help: Global mobility among professionals, especially students, has been growing rapidly over the last years. To give an example from my doorstep: In 2018, approximately 16,700 students studied at Maastricht University, with 51 % of them being international students (www.maastrichtuniversity.nl/education). You might object that this young Dutch university has given top priority to gaining international reputation since its founding days in 1976. But what about the following figures? In 2018,

- 13% of the 34,500 students enrolled at TU Dresden were international students, as were
- 15% of the 36,000 students enrolled at LMU Munich,
- 17% of the 28,800 students at Heidelberg University, and
- 21% of the 24,000 students at Free University of Berlin (www.timeshighereducation.com).
- In the same year, the Rhine-Waal University of Applied Sciences (founded in 2009) had approximately 7,300 students with 47 % of them coming from abroad (www.hochschule-rhein-waal.de/de)!
- In August 2018, www.mastersportal.com/countries/ reported Germany as the country with the second-largest number of English-medium Masters programmes (1,392) in Europe outside Britain, only outnumbered by the Netherlands (with 1,509 programmes), and followed by Sweden (879) and Switzerland (516).

Many smaller countries have long traditions of offering education in English or other languages than their official languages. The reasons for this are evident: being noticed by broader scientific communities, gaining access to better facilities and professional competition, attracting more, or more competent, international staff, etc. However, in the last few years, Germany has become a serious player in this game, too. This becomes even more obvious when we look at the dissimilar developments in the top three countries between January 2014 and August 2018: In the Netherlands, the number of English-medium Masters programmes "only" grew from 1,171 to 1,509, while in Germany (that was still third in position in 2014) the number almost doubled (from 765 to 1,392).

As a result, as an English-medium academic teacher in Germany at this time in history, you are likely to face a wide variety of students, with divergent cultural and educational backgrounds, levels, and varieties of world Englishes. And this phenomenon is likely to stay and grow.

Thus, as we have said before, you are challenged to enhance your listening skills and your intercultural competences, and to be aware of diverse experiences, expectations, and competences in your student audiences. And you need to make explicit your own expectations, standards, and approaches. In order to get *and* keep your students' attention, and to make them comprehend what you say, you need to use clear, understandable language.

It all has to do with *knowing your audience* and *choosing your language* wisely. When you see teaching in English not just as an interesting, replaceable method but as a means to enter real international academic discourse communities, you will not just have to speak differently but to *think* differently (cf. Reid 2010, 14).

Apart from the specific students in your specific class, this has to do with fundamental differences between continental European and Anglo-American academic discourse traditions. I am convinced that here are some of the biggest stumbling stones of switching to English-medium teaching. To make this clearer, please allow me to refer to *written* academic communication here, simply because it has been examined more thoroughly than spoken communication. As Natalie Reid explains:

> The rhetorical conventions of English, particularly academic English, contain a series of unwritten rules, the most important of which is that *the writer has to do all of the work*, so that the reader is essentially spoon-fed the information. The writer has to frame (i.e., introduce and contextualize) the entire paper, frame every section, frame every paragraph, so that the reader does not have to *think* as much as to simply *absorb* the information. The reader's job is to receive and consider clear writing, not to struggle with the words themselves to decipher the meaning. In other words, for academic writing, *English is a completely writer-responsible language.* (Reid 2010, 17; italics in original)

At the other end of the spectrum, there are the Chinese and Japanese linguistic cultures that place much of the responsibility for finding connections, drawing conclusions, etc., on the reader's shoulders. Most European rhetorical traditions are somewhere in the middle between these two extremes: They often allow or even encourage digressions, circular structures, etc., and leave it to readers to make their own sense of them. In English, such unlinear lines of argument may exist, too; however,

> (w)hile theories and theorizing are always welcome in English, they are welcome as long as the writer carefully introduces and presents them in a way that conforms to the expectations of an English-speaking readership. (Reid 2010, 17 f.)

In other words, *framing* plays a much more important role in many Anglo-American academic and scientific discourse communities than in their continental European counterparts. A US-American saying (based on ideas from Aristotle's rhetoric) puts it in a nutshell:

> First you tell them what you are going to tell them; then you tell them; then you tell them what you told them. (cited in Reid 2010, 18)

However, clear academic communication does not just result from a clear, explicit organisation of (written or spoken) texts. It is also closely related to simple, clear, and precise wording.[8]

I am well aware that for some European academic ears this sounds almost blasphemous. As somebody has said jokingly: The worst thing that could happen to a German scientist is to publish a paper that can be understood by non-experts… Of course, different research disciplines have different traditions.

8 The number of manuals for clear, plain academic communication in English is huge – and growing. Some of my favourites that focus on writing but also provide useful insights for spoken communication are Greene (2013), Reid (2010), and Douglas (2015).

But if you have been educated and have taught only, or mostly, in Germany or other continental European academic environments, you might agree: Sometimes, academic writers and presenters seem to be tempted to express their ideas in ways that make them sound *slightly* more complicated or impressive than they are.

Of course, I am exaggerating. I just want to stress how important it is for English-medium teachers to use simple language. Please get me right: I encourage you to avoid *overly* complicated language. I do *not* advocate oversimplifying things and using “Mickey Mouse English”, as one of my workshop participants once called it in disgust. On the contrary. As another famous quote often ascribed to Albert Einstein says: ‘Everything should be made as simple as possible but not simpler.’ I strongly support the use of concise terminology and some variation in general vocabulary (or other strategies to avoid boring your audience to sleep). You may have noticed that I have a soft spot for long sentences, too. However, being *overly* complex does not help: Actually, when you avoid *needlessly* long and complicated words, you might even be judged as being *more* knowledgeable (cf. Oppenheimer 2006)!

Clear is the magic word here. Well, one of the magic words. The other one is *appropriate*. Remember, we are talking about teaching. Unless you have good reasons to strive for something else, I firmly believe that clarity should be the leading principle in educational communication. And not only there, as Mark Twain stressed a long time ago:

> I notice that you use plain, simple language, short words and brief sentences. That is the way to write English – it is the modern way and the best way. Stick to it; don’t let fluff and flowers and verbosity creep in. (…) An adjective habit, or a wordy, diffuse, flowery habit, once fastened upon a person, is as hard to get rid of as any other vice. (Twain 1880)

To sum it up: Be brave, and use words as simple as possible, as appropriate for your specific course, your audience, and your communicative goal. By doing this, you become part of a tradition that has developed over centuries in many English-speaking countries and discourse communities.

Now, what do these general considerations mean for everyday communication at the academic workplace? To start with, I invite you to look at Paul Grice's classic Cooperative Principle. Grice states that talk exchanges are usually cooperative efforts, at least to a certain extent. Consequently, in order for such exchanges to work, participants are expected to observe this general principle:

> Make your contribution such as it is required, at the stage at which it occurs, by the accepted purpose or direction of the talk exchange in which you are engaged. (Grice 1989, 26)

This fundamental Cooperative Principle is divided into four categories. Grice calls them the maxims of

- quantity,
- quality,
- relation, and
- manner.

First, the *maxim of quantity* consists of two submaximes:

> 1. Make your contribution as informative as is required (for the current purposes of the exchange).
> 2. Do not make your contribution more informative than is required. (ibid., 26)

A well-known, much more recent acronym that expresses the same idea, is KISS, short for "*Keep it short and simple!*" (or other, less polite versions). As you may have noticed, I do not get tired of repeating "*as appropriate*" – which brings about the wonderful, friendly acronym KISS ASAP!

Second, the *maxim of quality* that refers to truthfulness is constituted by these two submaxims:

1. Do not say what you believe to be false.
2. Do not say that for which you lack adequate evidence. (ibid., 27)

While there are workplaces where saying the truth may not always be considered necessary or even professional, I am convinced that most people working in academia will agree that it is vital to say the truth (whatever that comes down to in their disciplines), and to make sure that what they say is based on evidence (whatever form this might take in their disciplines).

Third, there is the *maxim of relation*. Being both brief and true, it meets the criteria of Grice's first two maxims beautifully. It simply says: 'Be relevant.' (ibid.) It captures what I have been saying before: Every time you open your mouth in your English-medium classroom, consider the context, your audience, and your communicative goal for the day's session.

Fourth, the *maxim of manner* refers less to *what* is said and more to *how* it is said. Grice formulates it like this: 'Be perspicuous' (ibid.) Ironically, most readers would probably understand better what he meant had he replaced the word *perspicuous* with one of its synonyms such as clear, precise, explicit, lucid, comprehendible, or intelligible…

Anyway, its four submaxims make clear what he means:

1. Avoid obscurity of expression.
2. Avoid ambiguity.
3. Be brief (avoid unnecessary prolixity).
4. Be orderly. (ibid.)

This is not the place to start a discussion whether something like *necessary* prolixity (i.e., verboseness, wordiness, or lengthiness) exists at all… Grice's important message here is, again: Be as clear, brief, and organised as possible, to help your students learn and understand. Transferred to everyday teaching, the four maxims could affect the didactical strategies you use (see chapters 2.3 and 5.1), and which words and phrases you use (see chapters 2.4, 5.3, and 6).

More food for thought comes from the Plain English Campaign that started in Great Britain in the 1970's. The term *plain English* has been used for centuries to refer to the idiom of the common folk (mostly in contrast to Latin). However, in the second half of the 20th century, linguists started to use it for *clear, audience-oriented language*. According to Martin Cutts, an important promoter of the Campaign, communicating in plain English means

> [t]he writing and setting out of essential information in a way that gives a co-operative, motivated person a good chance of understanding the document at first reading, and in the same sense that the writer meant it to be understood. (Cutts 1995, 3)

He then expands on this definition (that basically rephrases Grice's Cooperative Principle):

> This means pitching the language at a level of sophistication that suits the readers and using appropriate structure and layout to help them navigate through the document. It does not mean always using simple words at the expense of the most accurate words or writing the whole document in kindergarten language … (ibid.)

Likewise, to advocate using English, particularly plain English, is not about sacrificing meaning to a modern *lingua franca* and, as a result, losing the diversity of national academic traditions. Some German scholars fear that the growing pressure to communicate and publish in English creates an Anglophone monoculture that reminds them of a return to scholastic times instead of fostering diverse, multilingual academic cultures and traditions (cf. Thielmann 2017). I strongly agree that multilingualism is to be preferred over monolingualism. However, debating the theoretical, political, and economic foundations of English-medium teaching is beyond the scope of this book. For now, it is good to remember that in most cases we are not talking about completely replacing a country's first language in the entire tertiary-education system with English but about adding one, or a few, English-medium classes to an institution's course offer.

In your own English-medium lecture or seminar, using plain English simply means that you adhere to a few principles:[9]

- Think before you say something: Who is your audience? What is the situation and which register is appropriate for it? What are your communicative goals in this particular situation?
- Prefer plain words. When you can choose between two words, choose the simpler one. Unless you have to use terminology to refer to a specific idea, phenomenon, procedure, or object, use short, well-known words rather than long, technical, unknown ones. Do not be afraid that being clear means you have to be unsubtle, or will be perceived by your audience as less competent, eminent, or academic. As Cutts (1995, 26) points out, odds are good that your listeners (and this includes academically educated listeners!) will find your contributions not only clearer, but also more organised, interesting, and stimulating.
- Omit needless words. Needless words include repetitions, excess detail, and wordy phrases.
- Use shorter sentences. This does *not* mean you should use telegraph style. It means to aim at an average sentence length of 15-20 words. It also means: Vary the length of your sentences.
- Put old, or known, information at the beginning of a sentence, new information at the end. When you do this, you effectively support your audience in decoding, grasping, and

9 Cf. Cutts (1995) and Greene (2013).

remembering previously unknown information. This strategy is important in written texts but even more so in complex spoken communication where listeners cannot go back to reread a previous section when they have missed a point.

- Tell a story. Telling and listening to stories is inherent to being human, and (as one of my favourite writers on the subject points out), story-telling is a powerful communicative strategy in academia to share ideas and connect with audiences (cf. Schimel 2012). In practice, this means:
  - Develop a clear, coherent structure for your lecture or presentation, or series of lectures.
  - Guide your listeners through your story by using transitions and signposting.
  - Favour vigorous, i.e., powerful, meaningful, significant verbs over nouns, particularly nominalisations. Favour the active voice.[10]
- Turn negatives into positives/affirmatives: Obviously, this is not to say that you should have a meaningless smile on your face all the time, or practise positive thinking. Rather, it is a grammatical principle based on neuroscientific insights: Most people's brains are much better at understanding affirmative formulations than negative ones (just compare "I love your presentation" with "I do not dislike your presentation"). Semi-negative sentence starters or double negations can be used effectively to stress something, but they are often

10 In my experience, the debate on using the active or passive voice belongs to the most fervent ones in academia. It is closely connected with academics' and scientists' identities. As there are no "hard" grammar rules on the correct use of the active and passive voice, you can do your students a great favour when you take a few moments to discuss the issue and to make explicit the conventions in your discipline. This will empower students to become more reflexive members of your disciplinary discourse community.

difficult to decode for listeners and readers (e.g., "Not until the 1990's did researchers answer this question." – When did researchers answer the question and is there an answer now?).

- Make lists, and make them parallel.

End of story.

Beware: Communicating in plain English is simple, not always easy. But it is definitely worth trying!

Time for reflection:

How can I be as clear as possible in my English-medium classroom? Which language is appropriate for my subject matter, my teaching role, my audience, and the setting (lecture, seminar, tutorial, etc.)?

What does Grice's Cooperative Principle imply for my particular teaching situation? How could I put into practice the maxims of quality, quantity, relation, and manner in my English-medium classroom more than I have so far?

What about using plain English, or *more* plain English? What is possible, desirable, and appropriate for me and my situation?

To whom could I turn to share experiences and to learn more about clear, plain communication in academia?

References and further reading

Bay, T. (2017). Don't make people feel stupid. Drop the jargon! Retrieved from https://www.rigzone.com/news/oil_gas/a/148966/Dont-make-people-feel-stupid-Drop-the-jargon on 19 August 2019.

Benjamin, A. (2013). Math in plain English: Literacy strategies for the mathematics classroom. New York/London: Routledge.

Cutts, M. ([4]2013). Oxford guide to plain English. Oxford: Oxford University Press.

Cutts, M. (1995). The Plain English Guide. Oxford: Oxford University Press.

Douglas, Y. (2015). The Reader's Brain: How Neuroscience Can Make You a Better Writer. Cambridge: Cambridge University Press.

dropthejargon.org.au is an initiative that promotes the use of plain language in community services and other workplaces (retrieved on 20 August 2019).

Greene, A. E. (2013). Writing science in plain English. Chicago: University of Chicago Press.

Grice, H. P. (1989). Studies in the Way of Words. Cambridge/London: Harvard University Press.

Oppenheimer, D. M. (2006). Consequences of erudite vernacular utilized irrespective of necessity: Problems with using long words needlessly. Applied Cognitive Psychology: The Official Journal of the Society for Applied Research in Memory and Cognition, 20(2), 139-156.

plainenglish.co.uk/free-guides.html provides many practical suggestions for communicating more clearly in Economics, Legislation, Health and Medicine, etc. (retrieved on 20 August 2019).

Reid, N. (2010). Getting Published in International Journals. Writing Strategies for European Social Scientists. Oslo: NOVA, Norwegian Social Research.

Schimel, J. (2012). Writing science: how to write papers that get cited and proposals that get funded. Oxford: Oxford University Press.

Schoerning, E. (2014). The effect of plain-English vocabulary on student achievement and classroom culture in college science instruction. International Journal of Science and Mathematics Education, 12(2), 307-327.

Thielmann, W. (2018). Eine erzwungene Einsprachigkeit wäre autokratisch. Retrieved from www.faz.net/aktuell/feuilleton/hochschule/englisch-in-der-wissenschaft-eine-erzwungene-einsprachigkeit-waere-autokratisch-15505823.html on 20 August 2019.

Twain, M. (1880). Letter to D. W. Bowser, 20 March 1880. Retrieved from http://twainquotes.com/Writing.html on 20 August 2019.

Wilkinson, R. & Zegers, V. (eds.). (2008). Realizing content and language integration in higher education. Maastricht: Maastricht University. Retrieved from http://digitalarchive.maastrichtuniversity.nl/fedora/get/guid:7a48d841-788b-44b1-add7-c0878081ffd7/ASSET1 on 7 August 2019.

Wilkinson, R. & Zegers, V. (eds.). (2007). Researching Content and Language Integration in Higher Education. Maastricht: Maastricht University.

William, J. & Bizup, J. (^{16}2016). Style. Lessons in Clarity and Grace. New York: Pearson.

5 Tips and resources for your own English-medium teaching adventure

Certainly, as an experienced teacher in your first language, you have over time collected and developed your own repertoire of teaching tricks and strategies. This chapter provides just a few more proven exercises and activities, ideas and suggestions to reach and actively involve students in those situations when everybody seems to be struggling with the twofold challenge of mastering content and language. The issues covered in this chapter range from strategies for activating students (5.1) to some basic ideas on how to use writing to facilitate English-medium teaching (5.2), and finally to online resources (5.3).

5.1 Activating students

Chapter 2.3 has already covered some fundamental didactical challenges for English-medium teachers. Following up on that, this section focuses on practical ways to activate students: lowering the threshold to speak in class (5.1.1), stimulating academic discourse competences (5.1.2), and giving students the freedom *not* to speak (5.1.3).

5.1.1 Lowering the threshold to speak in class

To make students feel more comfortable about speaking up in English-medium classes, you could *create opportunities for students to communicate in low-risk, low-exposure situations.*

One way to do this is to let students talk in smaller groups instead of the plenary. You could, for example,

- initiate and facilitate small-group discussions or reflections; when students discuss a question with a neighbour or two, this does not need to take longer than a few minutes. Answers and insights could be shared with the whole group afterwards – or not.
- start snowball discussions where students talk to a neighbour for two minutes, then get together with another pair, and then another group of four. Again, these small-group discussions do not have to take longer than a couple of minutes each, and you can add additional questions in each round to give students something to discuss.
- bring a playful or competitive note into the classroom by organising a "quiz show" (or less time-consuming, shorter task formats), e.g., to test students' understanding of subject matter, command of terminology or general academic language, etc.

Another aspect worth considering is the language you expect students to use in the English-medium classroom. Should you "force" students to use English throughout, even in buzz activities with their best-friend neighbour or in small-group work where they are surrounded by speakers who share the same first language? Studies on monolingual and multilingual approaches have shown that it can be effective to allow learners to code-switch, i.e., to use various languages. In content and language integrated teaching, to *allow or even encourage code-switching* makes sense for several reasons: It can boost students' confidence when they realise that while they are novices in your field, they can be competent in other areas of life. It can also signal that you let individual students learn and express themselves in ways that work *for them*, and that you respect and take seriously the personal qualities they bring into the classroom. Making several languages audible in class can make students aware that English-medium teaching is not an end in itself but aims to bring professionals with diverse backgrounds and experiences together to deepen everybody's understanding of the topic at hand.

Regarding content learning, allowing first-language use in class has proven to be particularly effective for tasks focusing on exploring, developing, and organising ideas. Students are likely to come up with different, and probably more interesting ideas because using their first languages enables them to draw on additional experiences and areas of expertise that may be connected to the subject only loosely.

If you want to engage students in lively discussions, they will probably talk more when you let *them* choose the language for small-group tasks. They may not speak English, but they will still discuss the content (and, of course, like in every classroom, some will not!…). When you ask each small group for a brief summary or report afterwards, they will have to translate their outcomes into English anyway. Alternatively, small groups could be asked to prepare mini stand-up presentations, interviews, panel or plenary discussions, debates, mini quizzes, etc.

5.1.2 Stimulating academic competences

Another approach to activate students in English-medium classes is to make explicit and to explain effective academic discourse strategies. When you provide students with opportunities to practise and refine their discourse competences, they will not only participate more actively in your own classroom; they will profit from it throughout their academic careers. Let us look at some ways to support students in *reading academic texts, asking questions*, and *giving presentations.*

To start with, it is well-known that many students can cope better during lessons when they have done some *reading beforehand.* In English-medium instruction, this is even more true. But how do you convince students that reading is an important academic skill in the first place? How do you encourage them to come to the seminar or lecture prepared? And how do you enable students who have been too busy to look at any of the suggested readings to take part in a group discussion?

- If you begin text work in small groups instead of the plenary, you minimise the risks of facing a completely silent student audience or making someone lose face.
- Guiding questions that point students towards particular text sections may seem unworthy of tertiary education in your eyes. However, remember the challenges many students in your English-medium classroom are facing, especially in their first years of study: Some of them are far away from home for the first time in their lives, and all of them try to master a new subject, educational culture, and language. You may feel like spoon-feeding them, but it might be the only way to engage students in discussions initially. As time goes by, you can empower them to become more focused, confident, and independent.
- Consider allowing (or even encouraging) reading texts in various languages. Could you let students read papers and articles in other languages they read more fluently than English? Depending on your field of research, does it make sense to encourage students to do some research and look for papers and books in other languages? This will certainly add new perspectives to the discussions on your subject matter. It might also make students more aware of how professional writers' first languages, and their decisions to write in specific languages, reflect cultural assumptions about academic writing and the subject matter.

Second, if we want to educate young people to be curious about the world, particularly their fields of study, we are well-advised to *encourage them to ask questions.* Most students find it helpful to be able to ask questions *after* lectures and seminars. However, some teachers are reluctant to offer this opportunity: They may find it unfair towards other students to answer individual questions, they may be fed up with answering the same questions again and again, or they may simply not be willing or able to spend hours in the lecture hall talking to students individually! One way out of these dilemmas could be to encourage students even more to ask their questions *during* lectures. Yes, this means that you need to be flexible as you may have to digress from your original plan. However, by the end of the lecture, more students might have understood what you wanted to convey. If you are familiar with teaching students from outside Europe, you know that culture-bound experiences and expectations may prevent some students from ever asking a teacher for clarification; after all, asking questions or even stepping out to a person who is higher in hierarchy could be regarded as disrespectful. Maybe it would be worth making such assumptions explicit and putting them in relation to your own expectations and needs in a Western-European academic culture? Instead, or in addition, you could think of ways to empower and encourage students to ask questions, for example

- pausing during lectures to give students time to look at their notes once more,
- giving students a few minutes to discuss their questions with their neighbours, or
- asking students to write down their questions so you can collect them at the end of the session and answer them in the next session.

In the English-medium classroom, be aware of the additional threshold that will make many students keep silent: their – perceived or real – low command of English. It may help if you do not just try to elicit student questions by asking something general like "Are there any questions about this?", or "Does anybody have a question?". (Someone has said that the latter is one of the most effective strategies to let a classroom full of students go silent within split seconds ...!) Rather, you could

- use *specific*, explicit, content-related prompts (as a bonus, this enables you to use technical language or terminology once more),
- provide students with general academic vocabulary, or let them create a glossary (online or offline), to enable them to ask questions without being distracted by language matters, or
- vary the questions you ask to activate different cognitive skills (e.g., knowing, comprehending, applying, evaluating, etc.), or affective dimensions,
- make students aware that you are not the only one who is responsible for what happens in the classroom but that they are responsible, too, or
- give students a few moments to write down their questions first.[11]

A third skill your students will have to master rather sooner than later in their academic careers is *giving presentations*. What about

11 Haynes and Haynes (2012, 138) describe what this could look like; and such approaches work in large groups, too: 'You could say: "Now I'd like to give you the chance to ask me questions about what I have just explained. You have half a minute in which to write down the question you'd really like to have answered, or a query you would like to raise. OK, I'm going to go along the third row back asking each person in turn to read out their question. So... What is your question?" Or, "Could you please turn to your neighbour and raise any question you have at this stage. Try and answer each other's questions. If you can't, write the question down. In two minutes, I am going to ask a couple of pairs what their outstanding questions are."'

making the English-medium classroom a practice ground? Here are some ideas for getting started:

- If your teaching format and group size allow for it, let students prepare mini presentations (and when I say mini presentations, I mean *mini* presentations: set a time limit of three minutes and make sure students observe it). When you stress that this exercise is about showing the "tip of the iceberg", not about trying to "lift the complete iceberg above the ocean surface", this can lower the threshold of speaking publicly on academic topics in English. Presenters apply new-learnt terminology right away, and the audience gets to hear different voices and accents in addition to yours.
- Ask students to stand up and give *unprepared* mini presentations, e.g., to present the results of small-group work. Let them collect ideas on cards and pin them on a pinboard, visualise their main insights on the whiteboard as they speak, or suggest other activities to get them moving and handling presentation devices other than a laser pointer.
- Invite students to give pecha kucha presentations (www.pecha-kucha.org): This means 20 slides, 20 seconds per slide, with no words on the slides. Some people find this a fantastic technique to avoid reinforcing spelling or other language errors on slides; it is also a good exercise for learning to focus – or to speak fast!

Whatever you choose to do to support your students to express themselves correctly, clearly, and confidently in academia, it will eat up some of your precious lecturing time initially. But in the medium and long run, students *will* perform better.

5.1.3 Giving students the freedom not to speak

To activate students by giving them the chance to remain silent sounds paradoxical. Let me explain what I mean by giving students the freedom not to speak, and why this can facilitate activation, motivation, and learning.

In some English-medium classrooms, everything seems to boil down to "functioning in English". But of course, other issues and competences are important as well. Students differ in how they learn and what they need in order to learn effectively. Respecting students' 'multiple intelligences' (cf. Gardner 2006), teachers could pay less attention to language every now and then and trust that students will profit from a session, whether they contribute verbally or not. For example, you could *offer several simultaneous activities* and let students choose how to take further a specific topic:

- Students with high levels of interpersonal intelligence could discuss questions in buzz groups while
- students with high intrapersonal intelligence could reflect on the same questions individually, and
- students with higher verbal-linguistic intelligence could produce a short text;
- students who are strong in logical-mathematical thinking could create a table or work with statistical data, and
- more visually/spatially oriented students could turn the session's outcomes into a visual representation (e.g., a diagram, mindmap, graph, illustration, academic scrapbook, etc.).

It may sound like a lot of additional work to prepare several "entrance doors" to one topic, but practice shows that this is not necessarily the case. Rather, you may find that you can relax and leave more responsibility for students' own learning processes where it belongs: with the students.

Exploring other communication channels than spoken language, you may also want to consider *making academic learning a more physical, here-and-now experience*. If you hesitate because you are afraid of bringing an inappropriate "touchy-feely" atmosphere into the classroom, here are some suggestions for low-level activities that have proven to work in academic environments:

- Use quick stand-up polls as warm-up exercises, to get students in contact with themselves, their peers, and the subject matter: Prepare a few yes/no statements linked to the session's topic and ask students to stand up when they agree. Then work with the small-groups that have emerged, ask students to elaborate on their opinions verbally, or use another follow-up activity.
- Where the setup of the classroom allows for it, encourage students to stand up and do a pair or small-group task with other people than their direct neighbours. This does not take a lot of time but is guaranteed to get students slightly – or very – puzzled, as they literally have to step out of their comfort zones to take different stances and to look at the topic at hand from new perspectives.
- Encourage students to leave the classroom. Start by giving them ten minutes to go for a short walk and ponder on a specific question, individually and silently, without looking at a screen as they walk. Or ask them to discuss a problem in pairs. Longer individual reflection and writing exercises can be done in other places outside the classroom, too. Admittedly, this works better in smaller groups and specific settings, such as whole-day courses. However, it is not a modern phenomenon: Even the antique Stoics proved the usefulness of this truly *ambulant* approach, at least for philosophers!

- Use voting technology (also referred to as student response systems or clickers) such as Socrative, Kahoot, or Verso. It allows instructors to ask questions and collect students' responses during lectures. This interactive approach enables you to get an impression of students' views and to incorporate them quickly and easily without students having to say a single word. For an overview of question types, activities, and challenges of using voting technology, see Bruff (2019).
- In some disciplinary contexts, it is possible and useful to include short experiments, even in large-group settings: Experiments enable students to physically experience ideas behind abstract theories or models and can impact student learning deeply.

A last way of giving students the freedom to stay silent in class is to create alternative communication channels and platforms. Blended learning enables students to discuss questions, give and receive peer feedback, etc., digitally. In the analogue world, cut short your lectures. Finish early on purpose to allow for individual questions and informal discussions. Of course, you will have to stick around if you want students to understand that you are not lazy but exploring new opportunities for communication! You could also arrive early and take time to chat with students before you start lecturing. In these slightly different settings, students who are not willing or able to speak in class (for whatever reasons) might step over the threshold and let you hear their voices, ideas, and opinions. As always, you decide what is most feasible for you and your students.

References and further reading

Bruff, D. (2019). Classroom Response Systems ('Clickers'). Retrieved from https://cft.vanderbilt.edu/guides-sub-pages/clickers/ on 23 August 2019.

Gardner, H. (2006). The development and education of the mind: The selected works of Howard Gardner. New York/London: Routledge.

Learn higher (n.d.). Free teaching & learning resources for staff in UK higher education. Retrieved from www.learnhigher.ac.uk on 24 August 2019.

Haynes, A. & Haynes, K. (2012). 53 interesting things to do in your lectures. Professional and Higher Partnership Limited.

5.2 Using writing to facilitate English-medium teaching

Developing routines helps to tackle many organisational tasks that accompany teaching. To write things down is *one* strategy many experienced lectureres find useful – once they sit down and actually do it. It can be tedious, and it takes time; but that is time well-spent as you do not have to start from scratch again every time you teach a subject, formulate assignments, give feedback, or explicate grading criteria. This effect becomes even more obvious in English-medium teaching: Written preparation is likely to make you more secure and knowledgeable in lectures, seminars, and individual meetings with students; many students, in turn, will find it useful to receive clear, written information from you. By distributing information in writing, you minimise the risk that students misunderstand or misinterpret what you say, or forget it again the moment they leave the room. On the following pages, you find some impulses for using writing to make life for English-medium teachers easier before, during, and after classes (5.2.1), and in office hours (5.2.2).

5.2.1 Using writing in and around the classroom

Depending on the communicative habits in your discipline, your student audience, and your content subject, you will be more or less familiar with, and enthusiastic about, written forms and teaching materials. Many teachers provide materials online, with students being responsible for reading them, or printing them out and bringing them to lessons. In English-medium teaching, providing written information beforehand can take some burden from you during the lesson itself as you do not have to make everything explicit orally and you have something to fall back to, if needed. The following ideas are simple and proven:

- For *preparing* lectures, upload reading materials and questions online beforehand to encourage students to reflect on certain issues, or to come up with questions in class.
- *During* sessions, visualise how they are structured, either in a classic list or table of contents, or in a concept map (Novak [2]2010), mind map (Buzan 2018), or – if you feel like letting off some creative steam – knowledge map (cf. Klare & Van Swaaij 2000 for the concept and for inspiration). As you put time and energy into creating such visuals, you may realise that it does not only motivate your students but also gives you new perspectives on your subject. Once you have provided a visual session plan at the beginning, refer back to it throughout the session. Many audiences appreciate being guided through lectures and presentations, as it helps them to stay focused.
- Together with your students, create a glossary for your course. This is an effective method to involve students and make them aware that all of you are learners of English, and that they are responsible for their own learning processes. At the same time, a glossary illustrates that the course contents are not given and fixed but that knowledge is defined

and constructed by discourse communities. Many students, especially first semesters, are not aware of the flexible, negotiable nature of disciplinary knowledge. A glossary could include general academic vocabulary (like the words and phrases in chapters 5.3 and 6.1), or only subject-specific terms and terminology. Agree whether you want to create a monolingual glossary (i.e., with English explanations and synonyms) or a bi- or multilingual one. It is also important to discuss who is responsible for compiling the glossary, and whether there are incentives and sanctions for students who contribute very actively – or not at all. You can use digital tools, online platforms, and social media to facilitate creating glossaries, either for specific courses and closed communities, or for broader audiences.

- Include short freewriting tasks in your lectures and seminars: Give students a few minutes, half-way through a session, or at the end, to write down their thoughts *quickly*, without thinking about logic, structure, or grammar – and *without having to share their texts* with anybody afterwards. Ask them to jot down, for example,
  - what they have found most interesting in the day's session,
  - what they have not understood,
  - what has annoyed them,
  - what they disagree with,
  - what has fascinated them,
  - what they would like to know more about, etc.

  Afterwards, give students another two minutes to share their findings in pairs, encourage them to write down and pass on to you questions they would like you to answer in the next session, or let this brief moment of written reflection stand alone.

- Similarly, insert one-minute writing tasks as a warm-up exercise at the beginning of a session or to lead students into small-group or plenary discussions.
- Support your students to take notes more effectively and efficiently. If you doubt that this is necessary, or *your* responsibility, just skip the next few pages. On the other hand, you may feel that sometimes during lectures, students concentrate more on taking notes than on listening to you, so they miss important information (cf. Airey & Linder 2006). If this sounds familiar, here are a few ideas (cf. Haynes & Haynes 2012):
  - Every now and then, ask students to swap their notes with their neighbours – they might find it quite eye-opening to see what their peers have written down, and how.
  - Invite students to focus on listening for a while and only allow note taking from memory after you have completed a section of the lecture.
  - Provide incomplete handouts to make it easier for students to pay attention to what you are saying and to take notes simultaneously. At the beginning of a course, you could go as far as including basic information, definitions, etc. As time goes by and students gain more knowledge on the subject, note-taking templates could contain more and more space for individual notes – a nice example of a scaffolded teaching and learning approach.
  - Provide audio or video recordings of your lectures.
  - Highlight crucial points verbally *and non-verbally* to draw students' attention to them.
  - Share your own notes (i.e., *real* notes, not a polished, almost ready-to-be-published document) to illustrate how content experts capture overall structures of topics rather than getting lost in details. Such examples, or models,

could be shared "live" during sessions or via online learning environments.

- Ask students to share their notes *with you*, so you can see whether you actually get your point across or may have to adapt your lecturing style, the amount of content you provide, the kind and number of handouts you prepare, etc.
- Explicitly ask students how you could support them, and what they could do themselves to take notes in English more efficiently and effectively.
- Encourage students to take notes in longhand rather than digitally. As many of them can write faster on the keyboard, they are tempted to record as many details as possible instead of trying to really understand the main parts of the "story". However, particularly for note taking, 'the pen is mightier than the keyboard' (Mueller & Oppenheimer 2014). (In addition, many people find it difficult to resist the temptations and distractions that come with keyboards and screens. No-screen policies have been seen to do wonders for concentration in many kinds of work-related gatherings…)

- Vary your approaches and give an example of the benefits of slowing down writing processes, and of writing in longhand: Use flipcharts, blackboards, and whiteboards instead of presenting spick-and-span powerpoint presentations. The classic method of developing illustrations step by step before the audience's eyes is still common in some academic disciplines for good reasons.
- When your classes are writing-intensive, take time to equip students for self-assessment and peer feedback on their own written work in progress. While text feedback can be provided digitally, many writers find that face-to-face feedback works even better. When you decide to work with peer feedback in a language that is foreign to most of your students,

be aware that it can reinforce mistakes, and that you might have to provide additional support and error correction. Make sure to clearly communicate and negotiate your own and your students' responsibilities – and the limits of these responsibilities.

- Encourage students to keep a professional journal/diary to record questions, new insights, and learning processes, both in and between classes.
- Consider working with learning portfolios in which students can record and demonstrate their skills, achievements, and learning processes over time.
- Finally, as for providing written information *after* sessions, the challenge is to find a balance between institutional requirements and ways to attract students to actually attend classes – and not only download the files.

References and further reading

Airey, J. & Linder, C. (2006). Language and the experience of learning university physics in Sweden. European Journal of Physics, 27(3), 553-560.

Buzan, T. (2018). Mind Map Mastery: The Complete Guide to Learning and Using the Most Powerful Thinking Tool in the Universe. London: Watkins Publishing.

Klare, J. & Van Swaaij, L. (2000). Atlas of Experience. New York, NY: Bloomsbury Publishing.

Mueller, P. A. & Oppenheimer, D. M. (2014). The pen is mightier than the keyboard: Advantages of longhand over laptop note taking. Psychological science, 25(6), 1159-1168.

Novak. J. D. ([2]2010). Learning, Creating, and Using Knowledge: Concept Maps as Facilitative Tools in Schools and Corporations. New York / London: Routledge.

5.2.2 Using writing in office hours

What has been said about providing written information in class is equally true for office hours: Taking the time for it once is likely to minimise miscommunication between you and your students, *and* saves you time and energy in the long run. You could start by

- collecting FAQs, i.e., the questions students keep asking in your office hours semester after semester. Write down your answers, put them online, and print out a copy and stick it to the wall next to your office door. Thus, your expectations and standards are clear, explicit, and easy to check for everyone.
- devising simple forms for individual or small-group office hours. Make them available online (and put a stack next to your office door) and tell students you expect them to bring a filled-in form when they come to your office hours. When students come prepared like this, discussions are usually more focused, goal-oriented, and time-saving.
- providing a form for students to take notes during the meeting – or to take notes yourself. When you make sure that both of you get a copy afterwards, you have a written record of what you have agreed on.

5.3 Online glossaries of teaching and education terms

The word lists and phrase collections below can serve as starting points for an online search to expand your active vocabulary for teaching in English. They could also form the basis of more specific, personalised glossaries (as suggested in chapter 5.2.1).

- The Cambridge English website provides several glossaries for teaching staff who would like to expand their knowledge of English for teaching purposes. For a general teaching glossary, check www.cambridgeenglish.org/images/22184-tkt-glossary-document.pdf (retrieved on 24 August 2019).

- The CLIL (Content and Language Integrated Learning) glossary on the same site (www.cambridgeenglish.org/images/22194-tkt-clil-glossary-document.pdf, retrieved on 24 August 2019) is more specific. The second part is particularly helpful as it provides vocabulary for referring to graphs and tables that can be applied in lectures and presentations.
- Educational techniques, and the language to describe them, have been compiled in this glossary of teaching and learning techniques for English as an academic language (EAL): www.pearsonschoolsandfecolleges.co.uk/AssetsLibrary/SECTORS/Secondary/PDFs/English/GlossarypagesfromEdexcelGCSEEnglishCoreTeacherGuide.pdf (retrieved on 24 August 2019).
- Most of the terms in the Glossary of Curriculum Terminology by the UNESCO International Bureau of Education will not be suitable for day-to-day use in the classroom. However, the glossary is a helpful starter and resource to reflect on many aspects of education in first-, second-, and foreign-language classrooms: www.ibe.unesco.org/fileadmin/user_upload/Publications/IBE_GlossaryCurriculumTerminology2013_eng.pdf (retrieved on 24 August 2019).
- Finally, Dunn's (2018) self-study materials for teaching in English do not just contain a German-English glossary; they also provide many exercises for improving educational and general academic language.

References and further reading

Cambridge Assessment English (2019). Language for Teaching. Retrieved from www.cambridgeenglish.org/teaching-english/teaching-qualifications/institutions/language-for-teaching/ on 30 August 2019.

Dunn, A. (2018). Lehre in der Fremdsprache. Teaching in English. Bonn: Deutscher Akademischer Austausch Dienst / Internationale DAAD Akademie. Retrieved from www.daad-akademie.de/service-und-downloads/downloads/de/69872-neu-ida-selbstlern-materialien-lehre-in-der-fremdsprache-teaching-in-english/ on 23 August 2019.

6 Useful words and phrases

This final chapter is a phrasebank, no less and no more. Of course, you could look up all these words and phrases yourself, online or offline. Moreover, I am convinced that most, if not all, words on the following pages are safely nestled somewhere in your memory. However, sometimes you may not have the time, or simply may not *want* to, look up English words and phrases to shift them from passive to active vocabulary. This is why this chapter has been included as a reminder and reference. It moves from vocabulary for aligning what you teach, assign, and assess (6.1) to phrases for classroom management (6.2) and oral exams (6.3).

6.1 Vocabulary to align teaching, assigning, and assessing

Chapter 2.4 has touched upon the importance of aligning teaching with assignments and assessment. To align your desired learning outcomes with what you teach, what you ask students to do in exams, and how you assess these exams, you need to choose the correct words. This section provides a list of typical, useful verbs for these purposes.

Obviously, not all the verbs mentioned here are suitable for *every* subject matter, genre, audience, and communicative goal. The best way to raise awareness of which verbs are needed, and conventionally used in specific disciplinary contexts, is to *analyse real texts from particular fields of research*. When you encourage students to "put off their content glasses" and "put on their language glasses" every now and then, you can help them to develop a deeper understanding of how language is used in *your* discipline's discourse community. When students are explicitly trained and adopt a habit of analysing language *in use*, they will realise that this is much more useful for vocabulary development than looking up synonyms in a thesaurus. Students need to realise that most synonyms are not identical but mean *different* things. The differences may be subtle, but they exist: A word's meaning may even vary depending on who uses it and in which context. As students become more aware of this, they can become more proficient academic presenters and writers in the discipline.

In teaching contexts, it is particularly important to use the correct verbs that *exactly* express what you want and expect from students. Certainly, few first-language teachers would search for synonyms just for the sake of variation. If they spent brain power on word choice at all, they would ask themselves which word expressed what they wanted to say most effectively. The same holds true in English-medium tertiary instruction. So ask yourself what your priorities are. My guess is that you will agree that expanding your academic vocabulary is just a means to an end, not the end itself. Have this in mind when you work with the table below, with verbs whose meanings are often *similar, but not exactly identical:*

levels of Bloom's cognitive knowledge domain	corresponding verbs
remembering	arrange, define, describe, duplicate, identify, know, label, list, match, memorise, name, order, outline, recall, recognise, relate, repeat, reproduce, select, state, etc.
understanding	classify, comprehend, convert, defend, describe, discuss, distinguish, estimate, explain, express, extend, generalise, give an example, identify, indicate, infer, interpret, locate, paraphrase, predict, recognise, rewrite, review, select, summarise, translate, etc.

levels of Bloom's cognitive knowledge domain	corresponding verbs
applying	apply, change, choose, compute, construct, demonstrate, discover, dramatise, employ, illustrate, interpret, manipulate, modify, operate, practise, predict, prepare, produce, relate, schedule, show, sketch, solve, use, write, etc.
analysing	analyse, appraise, break down, calculate, categorise, change, chart, compare, compute, contrast, criticise, deconstruct, differentiate, discriminate, distinguish, examine, experiment, identify, illustrate, infer, interpret, model, outline, point out, question, relate, select, separate, solve, subdivide, test, write, etc.
evaluating	appraise, argue, assess, attach, choose, compare, conclude, contrast, criticise, critique, defend, describe, discriminate, estimate, evaluate, explain, interpret, judge, justify, predict, rate, recommend, relate, summarise, support, value, etc.
creating/synthesising	arrange, assemble, attach, categorise, collect, combine, compile, comply, compose, construct, create, develop, design, devise, explain, formulate, generate, hypothesise, invent, modify, organise, plan, prepare, rearrange, reconstruct, relate, reorganise, revise, rewrite, set up, summarise, synthesise, tell, write, etc.

References and further reading

Bloom's Taxonomy Action Verbs (n.d.). Retrieved from www.marquette.edu/assessment/includes/documents/BloomsTaxonomyActionVerbs.pdf on 24 August 2019.

Bloom's Taxonomy Action Verbs (n.d.). Retrieved from www.missouristate.edu/assets/fctl/Blooms_Taxonomy_Action_Verbs.pdf on 24 August 2019.

Huitt, W. G. (2011). Bloom et al.'s Taxonomy of the Cognitive Domain. Retrieved from www.edpsycinteractive.org/topics/cognition/bloom.html on 24 August 2019.

6.2 Phrases for classroom management

Which words and phrases you need and *actually* use for classroom management depends on many factors. These include the specific teaching situation, the student population, the group size, personal communication styles, etc. You might feel that some of the phrases on the following pages would not be appropriate for your tertiary-education audiences and settings. However, both subject matters and teaching styles vary considerably from discipline to discipline, and from individual to individual, and what you consider infantile or otherwise inappropriate might be totally acceptable for somebody else in a different context. And remember: All these words and phrases that facilitate teaching and classroom management are meant to *make things clearer* for students, not to impress or – even worse – confuse them. So once more, dare to embrace simplicity, and pick the words and phrases that express exactly what you want to say, in a way that you are comfortable with.

Useful phrases for welcoming students and starting sessions:

- Good morning/afternoon/evening, everybody.
- Hello, everyone.
- My name is …
- This lecture deals with …
- This semester, we will …
- In this lecture/seminar/tutorial, we will …
- I expect you to …
- I look forward to discussing/exploring with you …
- Alright, let's begin.
- Shall we begin?
- Is everybody ready to start?
- I think we can start now.

- Now, let's get down to work.
- Let's get started.
- Are you ready?
- Are you with me?
- Let's just recap what we did last week.
- What were the main things we worked on last week?
- Any questions before we start?

Of course, students will talk to you and ask questions, too. You may find yourself having to react to sentences such as these:

- Can you say that again, please?
- Could you repeat that, please?
- Can you explain that a bit more, please?
- What does … mean?
- Sorry, I don't/didn't understand that.
- What is … in [German], please?
- What's the [German] word for …?
- How do you say this in [German]?
- Can you tell me another word for …?
- What about …?
- Can you write it on the blackboard/whiteboard, please?
- I'm afraid I can't see the blackboard/slide properly.
- Could you move over a little?
- Could you push the blackboard up/down?
- Can you speak louder, please?
- Would you turn the volume up/down, please?
- Can you switch on/off the light?

Useful phrases for reacting to student requests:

- Like this?
- Is this OK?
- I'm afraid I can't speak any louder.

- I seem to be losing my voice.
- I'm afraid I have a sore throat today.
- I'm sorry, but I can't move the screen.
- Does anybody know how to handle this?
- Would somebody switch on the lights, please?

Useful phrases for asking students to repeat what they have said:

- Pardon?
- Excuse me, what did you say?
- One more time, please.
- Could you say that again, please?
- Sorry, I couldn't hear that. Could you speak up a bit, please?
- Sorry, I couldn't hear that very well. Could you repeat it a bit louder?
- Sorry, I didn't hear the last part of your question. Could you repeat that part again, please?
- Sorry, I couldn't hear all of your questions. Did you say/ask ...?
- Pardon? I couldn't quite hear the last part of the sentence. Are you asking whether/if ...?

Useful phrases for checking understanding and for reacting to student questions:

- Sorry, I didn't understand the question. Could you repeat it, please?
- Sorry, I didn't quite catch your question/meaning there.
- Sorry, I couldn't understand the last part (of your question).
- Sorry, I'm not sure (that) I understand. Did you say/ask/mean ...?
- Sorry, I'm not quite sure of your question. Are you asking if/whether ...?

- Could you give me your thesis in one sentence, please?
- Is it your position that …
- To be clear, you're saying that …
- I'm confused when you say … Can you elaborate?
- Put another way, you're saying …
- So you're saying that …
- Is it fair to say that you believe …
- I hear you saying that …
- Sorry, I don't understand.
- I'm afraid I still don't get it.

Useful phrases for delaying or avoiding answering, and for giving tentative answers:

- Good question. Well, …
- Good point. Well, …
- That's a good/interesting question. OK, …
- Ah, yes. OK, that's a good point …
- (Now) That's an interesting question. You know, …
- Ah, that's interesting. Let me think (a second) …
- Well, you see …
- Now, let me see.
- Just a moment/second.
- How shall I put it?
- What's the word for it …
- Now, let me think …
- Let me get this right …
- Let me consider the best way to answer that.
- That point deserves some thought. Let's see …
- It's on the tip of my tongue.
- I haven't thought about that before, but thank you for your effort! I'll look into this.

- I am not familiar with this theory/idea/work, but I will look into that and let you know next week.
- Thank you for asking. Let's get back to this later, shall we?
- I'm afraid I don't know, but maybe someone else does?
- Is there anybody else who'd like to react to that?
- Anybody here who'd like to answer that?
- Ideas? Anyone?
- My first thoughts are that …
- Off the top of my head (maybe) …
- Don't quote me on this, because I might change my mind, but I think …
- That's a bit beyond the scope of today's topic, but my understanding is that basically …
- Let me sketch some thoughts (and maybe we can follow up after) …
- I'm not sure that's correct, but I'll look it up and we can discuss it later.

Useful phrases for asking for opinions:

- What do you think of …?
- What do you think about …?
- How do you feel (about …)?
- What do you reckon (about …)?
- What's your opinion of …?
- What are your views on …?
- Where do you stand (on …)?
- What would you say to … / if we …?
- Are you aware of …?
- Why do you think this happened?

Useful phrases for expressing opinions:

- I reckon …
- I'd say …
- Personally, I think …
- What I reckon is …
- If you ask me …
- The way I see it …
- As far as I'm concerned …
- If you don't mind my saying …
- I'm utterly convinced that …
- In my humble opinion …
- I'm quite sure …
- I'm absolutely positive …
- I'm fairly/quite certain …
- It must be right.
- I know …
- It's definitely …
- You can be sure …
- I've no doubt at all that …
- I'm a hundred percent certain that …
- I'm (utterly) convinced …

Useful phrases for asking for help:

- Can I have a volunteer?
- I need someone to help me.
- Can you give me a hand with this?
- Would you help me for a second?
- Can I ask you a favour?
- I wonder if anybody could help me with this?
- I could do with some help, please.
- I can't manage. Can you help?

- Give me a hand with this, will you?
- Lend me a hand with this, will you?
- Could you spare a moment, please?
- For this, I need some help, please.

Useful phrases for encouraging students to play a more active role in class:

- Who would like to give it a go?
- Who has an idea how we could deal with this? Anybody?
- Any volunteers?
- Do we have a volunteer?
- Anyone else who'd like to give it a try?
- Are there any questions?

Useful phrases for disciplining and confronting students:

- Can I have your attention, please?
- Could we have a little less chat, please.
- Would you stop talking, please.
- Would you please be quiet?
- Would you please stop what you're doing and listen for a moment?
- I'm sorry, but I can't accept such work.
- I'm not going to accept such behaviour.

Useful phrases for managing individual or small group work:

- Would you please make groups of four.
- Please move your desks into groups of six to eight people.
- Please put your desks in a horseshoe shape.
- The idea of this exercise is for you to …
- Please work together with your neighbour.

- Please find a sparring partner for this task.
- Find a new partner to work with.
- Please work in pairs/threes/fours/fives.
- Work in groups of two/three/four.
- I want you to form groups.
- Form groups of three, please.
- Here is a task for you to work on in groups of four.
- There are too many in this group.
- Would you please join the other group?
- Only three people in each group.
- I asked for groups of four people.
- I'd like everybody to work on this individually for a few minutes.
- Please work by yourselves.
- Work independently.
- If necessary, ask your neighbour for help.
- Please work on the task together.
- See if your neighbour agrees with you.
- Compare your answers with the person next to you.
- Compare your results with your neighbour.
- Please stand up and find another person to work with.
- Discuss the questions in your small groups.
- How much more time do you need for this?
- Remember to time yourselves.
- Keep an eye on time.
- You have another five minutes.
- You only have a few minutes left.

Useful phrases for giving instructions:

- Would you pass around the list, please.
- Whose turn is it to present / take minutes today?
- I think it's your turn, [name].

- Would you distribute these papers, please?
- Take one between two, please.
- You will have to share, I'm afraid.
- Turn to page [number], please.
- If you don't understand, feel free to ask me any time.
- Please swap/exchange papers with your neighbour.
- Would you please keep your questions for the discussion later?
- Please remember to bring … next week.

Useful phrases for managing time:

- Hang on a moment.
- Just hold on a moment.
- Just a moment, please.
- Excuse me for a moment.
- I'll be back in a moment.
- Please carry on with the small group exercise while I'm away.
- Are you all ready?
- First of all, today, …
- Right. Now we will move on to the next exercise.
- Have you finished?
- Let's move on to the next activity.
- Let's move on to something else.
- I think it's time to turn to our next topic.
- Maybe one more question before we turn to the next topic on our agenda for today?
- We still have a couple of minutes left.
- We seem to have finished early.
- We have an extra five minutes.
- We'll do the rest of this chapter next time.
- We'll finish this exercise in the next session.
- We'll continue with this next week.

And finally, useful phrases for ending sessions:

- That's all for today.
- One more thing before you go.
- It's almost time to stop.
- I'm afraid it's time to finish now.
- We'll have to stop here.
- Thank you for your good questions.
- For next week, please read …
- Please prepare the next chapter for Monday.
- Goodbye, everyone.
- See you again next Wednesday.
- Have a good holiday.
- Enjoy your vacation.

References and further reading

Deller, S. & Price, C. (2007). Teaching other subjects through English. Oxford: Oxford University Press.

Jones, C. (2017). How to handle difficult Q&A moments with confidence and professionalism. Retrieved from https://thinkscience.co.jp/en/articles/how-to-handle-difficult-QandA-moments.html on 24 August 2019.

International House Bristol (2018). Useful Expressions. Retrieved from www.ihbristol.com/useful-english-expressions/ on 24 August 2019.

Finch, Andrew (n.d.). Welcome to the classroom English page. Retrieved from www.finchpark.com/courses/links/classroom.htm on 30 August 2019.

Pérez Cañado, M.L. & Ojeda-Pinar, B. (2018). Communicative Classroom Language for Bilingual Education: Teaching 'Real English' for CLIL. Bern / Berlin / Bruxelles / New York / Oxford: Peter Lang.

Raizen, E. (2010). Foreign Language Teaching Methods: Classroom Management. Retrieved from https://coerll.utexas.edu/methods/modules/classroom/ on 30 August 2019.

6.3 Oral exams: basic considerations and useful phrases

When we talk about useful *phrases* for oral exams, it is a good idea to first recapitulate typical *phases* of exams, and the communicative situations examiners and candidates will and may run into. You will certainly realise that – apart from subject-related terminology, of course – the words and phrases for exams are not so different from the ones used in class. However, there are some slight differences that deserve attention.

So, what is likely to happen in an oral exam? Typically, oral exams can be divided into three major phases with different communicative responsibilities for examiners and candidates:

1. setting the scene,
2. facilitating examination, and
3. wrapping up.

Let us zoom in on these phases one by one.

6.3.1 Setting the scene

In the first moments of oral exams, examiners are responsible for setting the scene. As they are the hosts, they are responsible for everything a good host does: welcoming all people present, and making sure they feel as comfortable as possible. Typically, this includes introducing everybody to each other and informing everybody about organisational aspects, and their respective tasks and responsibilities. Examiners might offer candidates a glass of water or some other drink, and break the ice with a little bit of small talk.

Useful phrases for greeting candidates and introducing present colleagues:

- Good morning / good afternoon / good evening.
- Welcome.
- Hello, [name].
- Please come in.
- Have a seat.
- Would you like something to drink?
- Would you like a glass of water?
- Let me introduce my colleague, Ms/Mr [name], to you. She/He will be taking the minutes.
- You know Professor [name], don't you? She/He joins us as a part of our faculty staff and may ask questions as well.

Useful phrases for recapping procedures, and for inviting candidates to start:

- Let me briefly recapitulate our procedure.
- As we agreed on, you will start with a statement on a topic of your choice.
- Then, we will have fifteen minutes for questions.
- When the exam is over, you will leave the room, and the three of us will discuss the grade.
- We could start by talking about …
- Let's talk about … first.
- Which topic would you like to discuss first?

6.3.2 Facilitating examination

In the core phase of the exam, examiners have many responsibilities. Above all, they are responsible for structuring and facilitating the conversation; this means that they are expected to enable candidates to present themselves, their knowledge, and their competences as effectively and elaborately as possible. This is typically achieved by nonverbal and verbal expressions of agreement and positive reassurement that allow or even encourage candidates to interrupt examiners and to take the floor. In exam situations, the usual hierarchical settings and roles are reversed to a certain extent: Examiners are not expected to talk much but – on the contrary – to *make sure that candidates are put in the spotlight and receive as much talking time as possible.* Even when they disagree or get a wrong answer, good examiners do not start talking excessively themselves but challenge and prompt candidates to continue. When the candidates' incorrect or inappropriate answers lead to critical situations, examiners are responsible for overcoming such conversational crises, and for solving communicative problems. Finally, examiners should bring the exam to an end.

This wide array of communicative responsibilities shows that it is not exclusively in the candidates' own hands whether they succeed in an oral exam or not. Candidates depend *highly* on their examiners' willingness and abilities to give them a proper "stage" to present what they know. Against this backdrop, examiners are well-advised to prepare oral exams thoroughly, both individually and together with students; thus, both parties can agree on their respective roles and responsibilities in the exam and how they can cooperate to ensure that candidates perform at their best.

Useful phrases for letting candidates know that you are listening and want them to continue:

- Hm-hm.
- Right.
- Yes.
- Very good.

- That's very good.
- Good point.
- I like that.
- Marvellous.
- Fine.
- Quite right.
- That's right.
- That's it.
- That's correct.
- That's quite right.
- Yes, you've got it.
- That's a good point you're making here.
- That's more like it.
- That's much better.
- That's a lot better.

Useful phrases for expressing agreement and positive reassurement:

- I completely/totally agree …
- That's a good point.
- That's exaclty the point.
- You are absolutely right.
- Absolutely.

Useful phrases for expressing disagreement, partial agreement or doubt:[12]

- I completely disagree.

12 When you feel that you have to let candidates know that you disagree or doubt something they say in oral exams, make sure that your reactions do not silence the candidates; instead, explicitly *encourage and enable them to continue speaking and to display more knowledge*. For example, this can be done by asking for clarification or by providing more details (see below).

- I don't agree at all.
- No, you are missing the point.
- That's not the point.
- I can't see your point at all.
- But that's not always the case.
- But on the other hand …
- But at the same time …
- I see/take your point, but …
- I see what you mean, but …
- I agree up to a point, but …
- I'm not so sure about that.
- I'm not sure I agree with you.
- I'm afraid I don't really agree.
- I don't really think you're right.
- Not necessarily.
- Although I must admit that …, I wonder …
- Having said that, …
- It depends.
- It might be, I suppose.
- In a way, perhaps.
- Sort of, yes.
- Not really.
- Unfortunately not.
- I'm afraid that's not quite right.
- You can't say that, I'm afraid.
- Good try, but not quite right.
- Not exactly.
- Not quite right. Try again.
- Have another try.

Useful phrases for asking for clarification, and to encourage candidates to continue speaking:

- Would I be correct/right in saying that …?
- If I've understood you correctly, you're saying that …
- Am I correct in assuming that …?
- When you say …, do you mean that …?
- Are you saying that …?
- Basically, what you're saying is …
- I'm afraid I'm not quite/completely clear what you mean by that.
- I'm sorry, I didn't quite follow/catch what you said about …
- I'm afraid I didn't quite get/understand your last point. Could you go over it again?
- You were almost right.
- That's almost it.
- You're halfway there.
- You've almost got it.
- You're on the right lines.
- There's no need to rush.
- There's no hurry.
- We have plenty of time.
- Go on. Have a try.
- Have a go.
- Have a guess.

Useful phrases for providing more details to encourage candidates to continue talking:

- You referred to … Perhaps you could explain in some more detail how/what …
- This may sound like a stupid question, but I'd like to know …
- I wonder if you could help me. I'd like to know …

- I wonder if you could tell me …
- Do you happen to know …?
- I hope you don't mind my asking …
- Something else I'd like to know is …
- I wonder if you could elaborate a bit more on that last point?
- Could you share with us some more examples of …?
- Before we go any further, could you point out once more …

Useful phrases for interrupting candidates:

- May I interrupt you for a moment?
- Sorry to interrupt, but …
- If I may just interrupt you for a moment, I'd like to …
- I don't want to interrupt, but …
- Excuse me. Could I come in at this point?
- If I could just come in here, I'd suggest …

Useful phrases for shifting the focus to the next exam topic:

- So far so good; now, let's turn to …
- We are running out of time, so shall we turn to …?
- Well, why don't we talk about … for a while now?
- We haven't discussed … yet. Let's use the last five minutes for that.
- How about …?

Useful phrases for bringing the examination phase to an end:

- Our time is up.
- Thank you very much.
- Would you please leave the room for a few minutes now? We'll call you back in in a moment.

- Why don't you go outside and wait until we call you in again, so we have some time to discuss and agree on a grade.

6.3.3 Wrapping up

When candidates leave the room after the examination phase, examiners will usually take some time to discuss the grade with their colleagues. After this discussion, they will call the candidates back into the room and share the grade with them, explain and justify the grade, and congratulate candidates, as appropriate.

Useful phrases for calling candidates back into the room:

- Please come in again.
- Would you join us again for a moment?
- We are ready, so please come in again.

Useful phrases for sharing and justifying grades, and for congratulating candidates:

- Congratulations!
- It's my pleasure to let you know that we have agreed on a …
- We were all impressed by the way you …
- All of us agree that …
- We didn't quite agree on … Nevertheless, we think that for your overall accomplishment you deserve a(n) …
- I thought you had some weak points in …
- Although I wasn't quite happy with your argument that …
- Although I don't quite agree with you in that …
- I can see you've been working hard on …
- Your hard work over the last few weeks has paid off.
- You can be proud of yourself.
- I'm really impressed.

- I knew you could do it.
- Don’t worry, I’m sure you’ll do better next time.
- Practice makes perfect.
- You did a great job.
- Good!
- Excellent!
- Brilliant!
- Magnificent.
- Terrific.
- Fantastic.
- Well done!

7 Concluding remark

Congratulations – you have made it to the end of this book. And as it often happens in life, the end of one venture leads into the beginning of another, just as New Year's Eve is followed by January 1st, school is followed by admission to a university, and the previews are followed by the feature film. Reading this book may have solidified the methods you have used before when teaching English-medium courses. Alternatively, you may feel better equipped, and eager to implement some new ideas during your very first English-medium course this upcoming semester.

Wherever you are right now on your journey of teaching in English in higher education, I hope that you will keep celebrating the milestones you have reached so far, and that you continue your journey with professional courage and curiosity.

8 Acknowledgments

As almost everything in this earthly life, this book could not have been accomplished without the cooperation, support, and practical help of many people.

I am grateful to the numerous professors, lecturers, and instructors who have shared their experiences, opinions and ideas with me, and given valuable feedback on parts and early versions of this book. I also thank the staff at Narr Francke Attempto Verlag for their continuous professional support in the production process.

Over the years, many former and present colleagues in Maastricht, Bielefeld, and other places have engaged in lively discussions with me, worked with me as co-writers and writing mentors, and provided moral support. Special thanks go to Stefanie Haacke, Robert Wilkinson, and Clive Lawrence (†).

Thank you to my parents who have always challenged *and* enabled me to step out of the comfort zone and go the extra mile, literally and virtually. Thank you to Tim, Jelle, and Ronja, for being so patient with me whenever writing and teaching in English clash with daily family life. Thank you to Joachim, for listening to my complaints and wild ideas for endless hours, for encouraging me, and for never losing faith.

S.D.G.